Software Configuration Management

Macmillan Computer Science Series

Consulting Editor
Professor F.H. Sumner, University of Manchester

S.T. Allworth and R.N. Zobel, *Introduction to Real-Time Software Design,* second edition
Ian O. Angell and Gareth Griffith, *High Resolution Computer Graphics Using Fortran 77*
R.E. Berry and B.A.E. Meekings, *A Book on C*
G.M. Birtwistle, *Discrete Event Modelling on Simula*
T.B. Boffey, *Graph Theory in Operations Research*
Richard Bornat, *Understanding and Writing Compilers*
J.K. Buckle, *Software Configuration Management*
W.D. Burnham and A.R. Hall, *Prolog Programming and Applications*
J.C. Cluley, *Interfacing to Microprocessors*
Robert Cole, *Computer Communications,* second edition
Derek Coleman, *A Structured Programming Approach to Data*
Andrew J.T. Colin, *Fundamentals of Computer Science*
Andrew J.T. Colin, *Programming and Problem-solving in Algol 68*
S.M. Deen, *Fundamentals of Data Base Systems*
S.M. Deen, *Principles and Practice of Data Base Systems*
B.T. Denvir, *Introduction to Discrete Mathematics for Software Engineering*
P.M. Dew and K.R. James, *Introduction to Numerical Computation in Pascal*
M.R.M. Dunsmuir and G.J. Davies, *Programming the UNIX System*
K.C.E. Gee, *Introduction to Local Area Computer Networks*
J.B. Gosling, *Design of Arithmetic Units for Digital Computers*
Roger Hutty, *Fortran for Students*
Roger Hutty, *Z80 Assembly Language Programming for Students*
Roland N. Ibbett, *The Architecture of High Performance Computers*
Patrick Jaulent, *The 68000 — Hardware and Software*
J.M. King and J.P. Pardoe, *Program Design Using JSP — A Practical Introduction*
H. Kopetz, *Software Reliability*
E.V. Krishnamurthy, *Introductory Theory of Computer Science*
V.P. Lane, *Security of Computer Based Information Systems*
Graham Lee, *From Hardware to Software: an introduction to computers*
A.M. Lister, *Fundamentals of Operating Systems,* third edition
G.P. McKeown and V.J. Rayward-Smith, *Mathematics for Computing*
Brian Meek, *Fortran, PL/1 and the Algols*
Barry Morrell and Peter Whittle, *CP/M 80 Programmer's Guide*
Derrick Morris, *System Programming Based on the PDP11*
Pim Oets, *MS-DOS and PC-DOS — A Practical Guide*
Christian Queinnec, *LISP*
W.P. Salman, O. Tisserand and B. Toulout, *FORTH*
L.E. Scales, *Introduction to Non-linear Optimization*
Peter S. Sell, *Expert Systems — A Practical Introduction*
Colin J. Theaker and Graham R. Brookes, *A Practical Course on Operating Systems*
J-M. Trio, *8086-8088 Architecture and Programming*
M.J. Usher, *Information Theory for Information Technologists*
Colin Walls, *Programming Dedicated Microprocessors*
B.S. Walker, *Understanding Microprocessors*
Peter J.L. Wallis, *Portable Programming*
I.R. Wilson and A.M. Addyman, *A Practical Introduction to Pascal — with BS6192,*
  second edition

Software Configuration Management

J. K. Buckle, M.A., F.B.C.S.

MACMILLAN
EDUCATION

First published 1982
Reprinted 1985, 1987

Published by
MACMILLAN EDUCATION LTD
Houndmills, Basingstoke, Hampshire RG21 2XS
and London
Companies and representatives
throughout the world

Printed in Hong Kong

ISBN 0-333-33228-8

to my parents

Contents

Preface

Configuration management is a collection of techniques designed to improve the quality of software products by providing greater visibility, evidence of progress during development and production, and improved technical and management control. The term was originally applied to hardware development and production controls. Over the brief history of software systems the lack of such a control methodology has led to a number of well-publicised and costly disasters and it is in response to this that modern software configuration management has arisen. Many of the techniques are taken from the hardware experience, where a longer history has allowed good working methods to evolve; others have had to be developed from scratch in recognition of some of the unique properties and problems of software. Many are in fact good working practices that individual programmers apply to their own work without thinking, but that have needed to be extended and formalised to work with complex projects involving large numbers of people.

The application of configuration management, or CM, to software was pioneered by large computer manufacturers and specialised software teams working on large contracts, particularly in the aerospace and defence areas. As such, the procedures evolved tended to be relatively complex and comprehensive (TRW, for example, one of the leaders in the field, have a configuration management and software quality handbook some two inches thick [1]). Such complexity is of course entirely unsuitable for the average DP department project and, in any case, the environment in which work is commissioned in a DP department is totally different from that in which a major system contractor operates. Nevertheless, many of the fundamental ideas of CM are directly applicable to all software projects, providing they are suitably adapted to the different working methods. The author has practical experience of applying the methodology described in this book to situations as diverse as a major mainframe manufacturer's basic software, a special purpose mini-manufacturer's application software, the (large) DP department of a multi-national company and the four-man DP department of a sales company. In all cases there was a noticeable improvement in effectiveness and quality, which was actually more easily measurable in the smaller cases than the large ones. It is on this practical experience that the recommendations of the book are based.

The basic techniques described are equally relevant to: application software or systems software; commercial, scientific or process control; systems produced by computer users, manufacturers or software and systems houses. The way in which they will be applied will of course differ slightly, and the book is structured with this in mind.

The first two chapters of the book describe the overall aims and methods of configuration management and show its relevance and application in the areas mentioned above. Between them they establish the framework in which the individual techniques described in the rest of the book must be applied. Each of the remaining chapters describes an individual technique and is relatively free-standing. In total the mechanisms described will provide the methodology outlined in the first two chapters, but they are presented in the form of ideas, reasons and examples rather than as concrete procedures that all wishing to practise configuration management should obey. Examples are provided where possible but, within the limitations of a book this size, it is difficult to provide detailed case histories that are of general interest without giving also immense details of the background to CM operations in the organisations concerned.

Some guidance is, however, required on exactly how the principles of these chapters can be applied in practice. Appendix sections are therefore provided, each containing a skeleton procedure for the introduction of a particular control described in the main book. Each is based on an actual example that has been successfully operated by the author in one or more projects and is suitable for adoption by a project manager or group manager where it is agreed that the corresponding control is needed. Cross-references are provided to link the procedures to the relevant chapters of the main book, and indications are given of what modifications might be needed in particular circumstances. There is not a one-to-one correspondence between chapters and appendices, both since some techniques require several procedures and because the implementation of some of the configuration-management mechanisms is so much constrained by local circumstances that no general model is possible.

The book can thus be used in several ways

- as a method of updating the reader with modern software configuration management practice;
- as a source of ideas for introducing configuration management practices into existing control techniques;
- as a basis for building up a set of control procedures from scratch.

While, as stated above, the author has personal, practical experience of the successful application of each of the techniques described, he would be very interested to hear of readers' experience in implementing them in their own environments.

A selected bibliography on configuration management and associated matters is given at the end of the book for the reader who wishes to find out more about the history and practice of CM in software development.

Finally, three apologies. First, throughout the book the masculine pronouns and possessives are used for programmers, managers, etc. This is merely a shorthand for the more accurate, but much more clumsy he/she, him/her and his/hers. (Perhaps we should follow the Finns and adopt a single, sexless pronoun!) Second, although the history outlined above shows how the term 'configuration management' came to be applied to software, it is nevertheless in the author's opinion a highly confusing name. No doubt the reader could think of several better expressions for the control techniques described in this book. Unfortunately, particularly in the United States, the term has passed into common usage and to coin new names would only add to the confusion. Readers who, like the author, are upset by misuse of the language are advised to use the abbreviation CM and to let it stand for anything (control methodology?) or nothing as they think fit. Last, methods of controlling staff involved in software development and maintenance are not the most scintillating subject. As a result a book describing them is unlikely to make good bedside reading. Nevertheless, some degree of detail is essential if sufficient information is to be provided to allow the actual implementation of the methodology. More casual readers are asked to make allowance for this and, if they find themselves at any time less than enthralled, to skip to the next main subject area.

J. K. BUCKLE

Acknowledgements

The author wishes to thank TRW and in particular Barry Boehm, Director of Software Research and Technology, for permission to use their baseline diagrams in chapter 3, and the unit development folder details in chapter 9.

1 *Basic Configuration Management Concepts*

1.1 WHAT IS CM?

Configuration management, or CM, is the term used to cover a collection of techniques that, when applied to software development and maintenance, will improve the quality of the software product, reduce its life-cycle costs, and improve the management function for the development or production process. Configuration management is closely allied to, but different from, normal quality-assurance and quality-control techniques, and is mainly concerned with providing a foundation on which quality-control measurements can be made.

There are four basic planks in the CM platform

- *identification:* actually specifying and identifying all components of a software system; the form of their identification will change throughout the life of the project from outline specification to actual code;
- *control:* the ability to agree and 'freeze' specifications or actual code and then to make changes only with the agreement of appropriate named authorities; such change control allows all relevant factors and possible effects of a change to be considered before a change is authorised;
- *status accounting:* the recording and reporting of all current and historical data concerned with a program configuration;
- *verification:* a series of reviews and audits to ensure that there is conformity between a product and its appropriate identification.

The basic techniques apply to projects of all sizes, and to all stages of software development and production. However, the way in which they are applied can differ considerably both with the project type and team size, and with the stage in the product life-cycle.

A professional programmer will normally apply such techniques to his own work without thinking. He will, for example, name programs and program units, keep track of changes made, store old versions, and check the accuracy of his work at predefined points. What this book describes is the way of applying similar disciplines to projects involving more than one person.

1.2 BASELINES

The operation of configuration management for software development makes use
of the concept of *baselines*. A baseline is a well-defined point in the evolution of a
project from the statement of initial requirements to final availability. In the early
stages of a software development project, a baseline will correspond to a document
of some sort — a requirements specification, a design specification, etc. In later
stages a baseline will be a version of the actual software. With a CM system,
standard baselines are established for a project and successful completion of such
a milestone is established by a review or audit (verification). The baseline then
forms a foundation for movement to the next milestone. In order that it should
be a firm foundation it must be placed under change control — that is, subsequent
changes must only be made with the approval of the relevant authorities (control)
and all such changes are fully documented (status accounting).

This step-by-step progress is illustrated in figure 1.1. First the user needs are
analysed to produce a requirement specification. This forms the basis of an
analysis of the features that the completed system must possess to satisfy the
needs of the user, resulting in a functional specification. The next stage is to
transform this into a particular design that provides the required functions. The
design may be done in one or more stages (outline design, detailed design, etc.)
and leads eventually to a specification describing the detailed form of individual
modules, their testing and the integration and testing of the total system.
Implementation follows and the working system thus obtained needs to be made
operational. It is the properties of this operational system that should meet the
user needs.

In order that the user needs are met effectively it is necessary to ensure that
each step taken is a genuine step round the cycle and does not go off at a
tangent. This is done by the verification processes shown as lighter anti-clockwise
arrows. The requirements specifications must be verified against the stated user
needs; the system described in the functional analysis must be chcked to be sure
it satisfies the requirements; and the design produced must be validated against
the functional specification. From this point we are dealing not with descriptions
but with actual software that can be tested against relevant criteria produced at
earlier stages. The system components, subsystems and fully integrated system
are tested to specifications produced during the design. Similarly, the
operational system can be validated against the requirements. If all these
verifications are successful then the properties of the resulting system should
match the initial user needs.

It is interesting to note that there is nothing specifically peculiar to software
about this process. The diagram could apply equally well to a computer hardware
development or a civil-engineering project, such as a bridge, by changing the last
two pictures in the cycle.

1.3 INTERACTION WITH OTHER CONTROL SYSTEMS

Figure 1.1 also illustrates the interaction between CM and another control

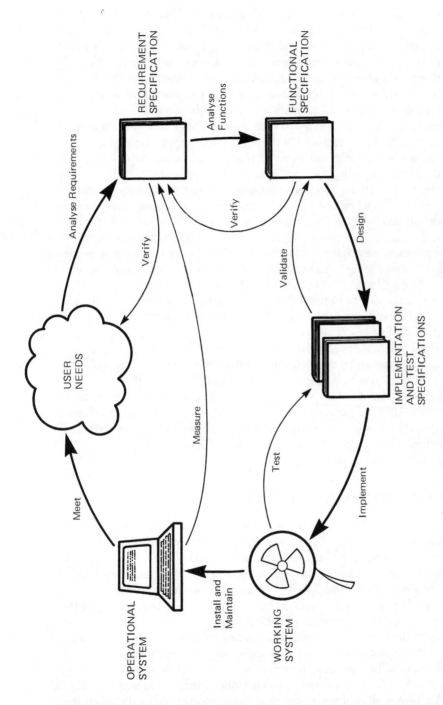

Figure 1.1   The system development cycle

system – quality assurance and control. Essentially, CM is concerned with providing firm measuring points from which quality can be assessed. CM must also be closely tied in with normal management review, control and planning systems. As an example, any standard milestones used in an organisation's management and reporting system, and the development phases that they define, should be compatible with those used in CM procedures. Again, any existing design review and acceptance-testing mechanisms should be considered to be foundations upon which other CM mechanisms can be built.

The way in which detailed CM procedures operate will also be very dependent on the tools used. In development, the language used, the integration methods and the testing tools will influence CM, while after initial development the methods of storing and generating improved versions or variants will have a fundamental effect on CM controls. Finally, all working computer systems are essentially hardware–software amalgams. For most DP installations the hardware does not change very rapidly but the basic software that underlies application programs may change frequently, and CM-type controls must be applied to keep the status of the total hardware–software system known and operational. In major developments, even in modest DP establishments, the hardware configuration may be changed to meet new system requirements. In all such cases it is advisable to use the same procedures for status recording and control of all system components.

Finally, note that CM is entirely independent of the methodologies adopted for the actual analysis, design and implementation of the software. Some modern analysis or design technologies help greatly with the implementation of CM by providing basic documentation and change control methods. They are therefore useful in earlier development stages. Similarly, sensible choice of implementation language and support tools will aid CM practices in later stages. However, the ideas of CM will work with any reasonable choice of technologies.

1.4 BASIC DEVELOPMENT CONTROLS

As stated in the preface, the aim of CM is to bring the methodology for the realisation of software into step with other engineering disciplines. This means improving control and measurement of quality, finance and timescales. It also means standardising methods to some extent, to avoid costly duplication and to allow ease of interchange of information. At first sight this may seem like just another bureaucratic overhead on the programmers. In fact it is just the opposite. Sensible application of the techniques of this book remove, or ease, many of the boring tasks involved in creating software systems, allowing the programmer to concentrate on the intellectual problems of design and construction. This can lead, in turn, to automation of the functions of organisation, tracking and remembering (which machines do well and humans do badly) and allow management and staff to concentrate on the things that really count.

Three main sets of controls normally apply to new developments

- technical: the need to provide certain functions within known technical constraints;
- financial: the need to keep to financial budgets and timescales for the development process itself, and to produce an end product within given price constraints;
- quality: to ensure that the quality of development is such as to meet user needs and to allow an efficient production or maintenance process.

For much of the time these controls may be considered separately, but they do interact. For example, we can often reduce financial costs of development by lowering technical requirements or reducing quality (and therefore possibly increasing production or maintenance costs). In most well-run software organisations, systems already exist to operate all three controls. In the CM area we are concerned not with replacing any of these systems, or even with adding to them, but rather with providing a simple underlying methodology that will aid the operation of these controls, co-ordinate them and attempt to hold or reduce the overheads on the project manager.

Section 1.2 explained the idea of a 'baseline': a milestone in the process of implementing a product, against which progress could be measured and which formed a foundation for future work. Any such foundation must be as firm as we can make it, hence the need to 'freeze' specifications and versions of systems at certain stages. ('Producing software from a specification is like walking on water — it's easier if it's frozen' — Barry Boehm.) Nevertheless, because development is by nature unpredictable, and because developers are human, there may be a need to alter such foundations at a later stage. Such changes must only be made after consideration of all the possible consequences and, once made, must be broadcast to all the relevant project staff. The system to control such operations is commonly called 'change control' and has been practised for years in hardware development and production. It is important that any software change control system is not too bureaucratic and, in particular, waiting for approval of a software change must not be a bottleneck to the development process.

The main tasks of the CM system in development, then, are as follows.

- specifying the baselines, and the documentation or systems that constitute them (configuration identification);
- specifying a multi-level change control system to handle the items that constitute the baselines (configuration control);
- making the status of baseline items and changes known to all affected parties and keeping records down to the level of software 'units' (configuration status accounting);
- augmenting normal quality-assurance techniques to review and audit adherence to standards and progress towards completion (configuration auditing);

- integrating this process with existing technical, financial, quality and management controls (see, for example, reference 2);
- co-ordinating the total set of controls with the tools used during the development process.

1.5 POST-DEVELOPMENT CONTROLS

Even after development of a one-off software system the software does not stand still; bugs are found and fixed; enhancements are requested, scheduled and made; systems are lost and need to be regenerated. During this period, which will normally be much longer than the development period, staff will almost certainly change and, even for unchanged staff, memories will fade. In such circumstances, it is, if anything, even more important that errors are recorded, changes are controlled, all changes are recorded, backups are kept and documentation is kept in step with the actual software. In cases of major change to an existing system, the work can be considered as a redevelopment and the CM development methodology is equally applicable.

In cases where a software system is to be installed on more than one site, other concerns appear. The systems must be kept in step, or variations and their reasons well documented. More complex error-recording and error-correction systems will be needed, and various levels of corrections may be required: quick-fixes by code or data patch, source corrections, reissues, etc. The control, recording and verification procedures necessary for this type of software production are also covered by CM techniques, and are dealt with as mechanisms in later chapters.

1.6 THE STRUCTURE OF THE BOOK

The next chapter outlines the general framework of software development, and isolates those areas that require configuration management control. Each of the mechanisms necessary to provide this control is then described in detail in subsequent chapters as follows.

Chapter 3: Baselines

A baseline is a milestone in the process of implementing a product, against which progress can be measured, and which forms a foundation for further work.

Chapter 4: Configuration Identification

This section deals with rules for naming and registering software items and applying them to all components coming under CM control.

Chapter 5: Document Production and Document Change Control

It is necessary to have a formal method for producing and agreeing specification documents and, after agreement, to change them only under control, with due regard to all the possible effects of such changes.

Chapter 6: Code Change Control

Changes to accepted code must also be controlled and kept in step with documentation changes.

Chapter 7: Reviews and Inspections

To monitor the quality of software at points before the completion of the system involves the use of methods for critically assessing design and development at an early stage.

Chapter 8: Testing and Validation

While quality assurance is a separate methodology, quality requirements do have CM implications and these are dealt with here.

Chapter 9: Internal Documentation

Careful planning and standards can permit the generation of internal documentation simultaneously with the design and implementation of the system, with only small overheads on the main process.

Chapter 10: Maintenance and Production

Software maintenance begins with a formal handover from development, and it is essential that at this point the product is capable of being maintained, and that trained people and adequate tools and documentation exist to allow this to take place. After handover, the resulting system will always need some support. This requires error processing and recording systems, statistics gathering, user publications and possibly reissue systems.

Chapter 11: Use of Tools

The use of well-designed tools can provide many of the controls necessary for configuration management without great overheads.

Chapter 12: Organisation for CM

This section deals with the introduction and establishment of CM procedures within an operational group.

Software configuration management has evolved in the area of very large systems — military and space developments, for example. As such, while the basic ideas are equally applicable (and equally vital) to small systems, adoption of the full majesty of a major CM system would not only mean an unacceptable overhead but also a distinctly demotivating influence on staff. For that reason, while the majority of the book deals with the most complex cases, at the end of each relevant chapter a short section is devoted to the customisation of the concepts that is needed for simpler projects. That this custom-isation is possible is proved by examples such as that reported in reference 17, where techniques similar to those advanced here were applied successfully to a one-semester student project.

Even where the size of a project justifies adoption of the complete methodology, many of the individual procedures and operations will need to be tailored to the application. It is therefore necessary for project managers and relevant management and review staff to decide what configuration management standards are appropriate to a particular product, and to adapt and apply them accordingly. This flexibility allows great freedom to those in charge to run their teams in the way they find most convenient; it brings with it the associated responsibilities of considering carefully from the outset how CM is to be applied, and of enforcing these standards throughout.

2 Configuration Management Mechanisms

Subsequent chapters are concerned with mechanisms — that is, the tools and methods that can be used to apply configuration-management techniques to software development and production. They do not, in general, attempt to describe detailed methods — this is reserved for appendix B — but rather explain the underlying concepts and reasons. Some techniques and tools are equally applicable to both development and post-development phases, while others are more specialised for one activity or the other. Both types of mechanisms are discussed.

Within any organisation the maintenance of specific CM procedures must be an on-going process. This is both because requirements will change over time and because initial proposals for procedural standards, such as appear in the appendices of this book, will be improved with usage. Nor is it always possible to apply all procedures indiscriminately to all projects, although special methods developed for single projects may find their way into the general standards for an organisation. Again, while most CM procedures can be operated manually, one would expect that, as CM operation increases, automated tools would be developed or purchased to support the procedures. Examples are text-processing systems for producing document variants and modifications simply but controllably, and test systems that can generate test programs or data and record which part of a product has been exercised and with what results. Such tools will increase the advantage of using the procedures that they support, although even with tool support it is not always possible to apply all procedures identically to all projects within an organisation.

The purpose of this chapter is to outline the classes of configuration management techniques and place them in the context of the overall product life-cycle. We begin by examining the basic activities that constitute a development project.

2.1 THE DEVELOPMENT PROCESS MODEL

In this section a diagrammatic model of the system development process is used as a basis for applying CM techniques. Figure 2.1 shows the process illustrated at the top level as an SADT^{TM} diagram. SADT is a structured analysis and design technique developed by SofTech Inc. and readers wishing to know more about

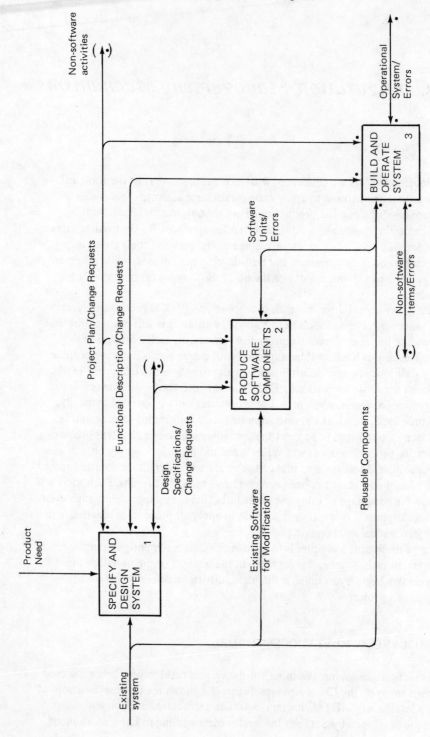

Figure 2.1 Develop a software system

it can consult reference 3. For our purposes it is sufficient to know that activities represented as boxes have inputs shown on their left, and outputs on their right. Arrows on the top of a box are controls.

The software development process consists essentially of three stages, each represented by a box.

(1)   'Specify and design system' is controlled by the need for a new product. The activity generates software design specifications, which control the activity of 'producing software components', and a functional description, which controls the activity 'build and operate system'. Changes may arise in the later activities that cause a feedback, represented by the double arrows with dots. These will give rise to a reactivation of the earlier box. The initial activity also generates a project plan that controls all subsequent activities, including non-software activities that are not detailed on this diagram (the arrowhead shown in parentheses). Again, changes to the plan may be fed back. Finally, designs are produced for non-software system components, for example hardware, operations or data collection. This again is not the concern of the present diagram. Any existing system will be taken into account in the production of specifications.

(2)   Under the control of the software design specification, software components are produced and passed as tested units to the activity 'build and operate system'. Changes to the specification or plans arising from this activity are fed back to 'specify and design', while errors found in the 'build and operate system' can be reported back to the current activity, causing rework. Existing components may be used as a basis for new ones.

(3)   The activity 'build and operate system' takes the new, tested software units, any reused existing units and non-software components of the system builds a workable system. Errors are fed back to be corrected, and finally an operational system is produced. Errors discovered during operation must be corrected, and users must be supported.

For any particular development, some of these items may be null; for example, there may not be an existing system. It is important to notice that, while we are concerned here only with software configuration management, no system can consist of software alone: it needs hardware to run it and also people to create input and use output either directly or indirectly. It is the failure to consider such a total system that leads to poor end-user service, as demonstrated by many early banking systems. For organisations producing total hardware—software systems, of course, a complete parallel activity to box 2 is required for hardware development or acquisition.

Using the SADT technique we can decompose each of these three activities into its component parts using similar diagrams. If we then recombine these detailed diagrams into one we obtain figure 2.2, which covers the same activities as figure 2.1, but in greater depth. Names of documents and activities vary between

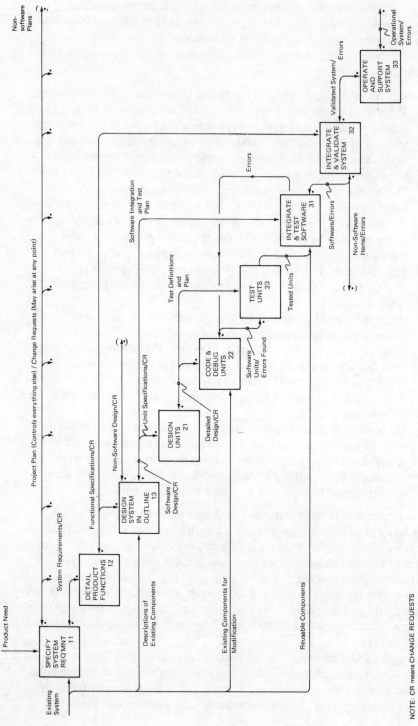

Figure 2.2   Develop a software system – details

NOTE: CR means CHANGE REQUESTS

organisations, but it should be possible to map most software operations on to this diagram.

We now have nine activities which between them take the 'product need' at the top left corner and from it produce an 'operational system' at the bottom right corner. These processes are as follows: figures in parentheses indicate the appropriate diagram box.

Specify System Requirement (11)

This process takes the needs and from them produces system requirements and an overall project plan. The output must include not only technical and functional requirements for the software and the total system, but also documentation requirements, validation requirements and such constraints as compatibility. The project plan will include not only timescales but resources and financial information. Change requests to both plan and requirements may be generated at later stages and must be dealt with in a controlled manner. Essentially the requirements document should be from an end-user standpoint, and is sometimes called a user, or user requirement, specification. Details of any existing system are used as an input to the process.

Detail Product Functions (12)

From the requirements, the necessary functions are determined and expanded to produce the functional specification. This includes all the relevant software information from system specifications, plus other constraints such as design and documentation standards, tools and languages to be used, etc. It may also include special tools needed and similar details for non-software system components. The testing and validation requirement will be expanded to describe the actual testing to be done, in conjunction with activity 13 below. Subsequent changes are dealt with under change control. Draft user documentation should normally be produced at this stage. (The functional specification document is sometimes called a development specification.)

Design System in Outline (13)

This activity generates a software design that satisfies the requirements and constraints of the functional specification down to unit specification or data description level. (A 'unit' may be a module or a group of modules depending on the project and tools used.) Some units may already exist or be obtainable from existing products. Others may be formed by the modification of existing units. Similar design descriptions are produced for other aspects of the system, such as hardware or operational procedures. The activity also produces a plan for the integration of all units, and test requirements to allow the tests to be prepared *before* completion of the system. The outline design may be changed under control.

Design Units (21)

For each unit specification a detailed design is produced; this may consist of flow charts, design diagrams, pseudo-code, data definitions, etc., but is, in any case, sufficient to allow coding to begin. Definitions of the tests required for the unit are also produced before coding starts. Controlled changes may be made to the unit design as a result of coding experience.

Code and Debug Units (22)

Units are coded and debugged ready for testing according to the test plan. Existing units may be modified to produce new units. Errors found in testing are dealt with.

Test Units (23)

Units are tested according to the test definitions and plan, and any errors passed back. Successfully tested units are passed on for integration.

Integrate and Test Software (31)

The tested units are put together and integrated according to the integration and test plan. Both newly developed and existing units are accepted in the same way. Errors found are fed back: new versions of units are accepted under control.

Integrate and Validate System (32)

Software and other developments are married and the total system validated against

- the functional requirements;
- the documentation requirements;
- adherence to standards;
- other constraints – size, speed, performance, compatibility, etc.

The output is a validated system that forms a basis for operational use. The system is 'handed over' for installation and support.

Operate and Support System (33)

The validated system is installed and used. Errors must be corrected and users supported. (Major enhancements are dealt with as redevelopments.)

It should be noted that the SADT diagram, unlike a flow chart, does not describe a sequential, time-based process. Figure 2.2, for example, allows for reactivation of earlier boxes in response to change requests and the CM system needs to deal with this. Examples of the non-sequential nature of the model are

- preparation of test programs and systems, and integration tools and systems that are part of box 31 can, and should, begin immediately after completion of the main activity of box 13;
- errors discovered in box 31 'integrate and test software' could, by the various feedback loops, give rise to any or all of:
  a coding change (box 22)
  a unit-design change (box 21)
  an overall software-design change (box 13)
  a change to software or system requirements (boxes 12, 11)
  changes to the project plan (box 11)
  a new integration and test plan (box 13).

2.2 CM IMPLICATIONS

The software development process defined in figure 2.2 implies certain areas where configuration controls and tools can be applied and where formalised procedures are necessary.

(1) Project initiation: at the start of a new project it is necessary to establish the framework of rules under which the development will take place. Some of the activities involved in this initiation will be covered by normal organisational standards; others are more CM biased and will be covered in more detail in this book. Of particular importance are the establishment of development baselines, the tools and methods to be used, the constitution and responsibilities of various review bodies, change control authorities and so on. Because initiation needs to consider all that follows, it is left until quite late in this book.

(2) Baseline definition: the statement of the various specification documents that define baselines; of the form they take and their contents; and of the form and content of baselines in the actual software. Obviously each of the major outputs of the boxes can be taken as a baseline. The idea of baselines for development was introduced in chapter 1. In the next chapter more attention is given to the actual form that baselines should take and the agreement process for them.

(3) Configuration identification: this involves augmenting any existing rules for naming, numbering and registering conventions, applying them to all components coming under CM control and ensuring that such information is available for all items, whatever their format or storage medium.

(4) Document production and document change control: particularly for specification documents that form baselines, it is necessary to have a formal method for producing and agreeing documents and, after agreement, to change them only under control, with due regard to all the possible effects of such changes.

(5) Code change control: once code has been accepted for integration into a

system and, more importantly, when it has been handed over to users, even superficially trivial changes may have large effects that are not immediately obvious to the person making the change. It is therefore necessary to agree and control changes to such code in a fashion analogous to the control of specifications. There is also a need to tie the two systems, to ensure that documentation and code are kept in step with each other and with any changes to hardware or support systems.

(6) Use of tools: the use of tools such as archives and test systems during development can, if properly planned, provide many of the controls necessary for adequate configuration management without generating overhead activities for the developer.

(7) Reviews and inspections: in the interests of reliable software development, it is necessary to assess the quality at points before the completion of the system. This involves the use of recently developed technology for critically assessing design and development at an early stage. Such technology is essential for the approval process that actually signifies achievement of a baseline.

(8) Testing and validation: this aspect of development is mainly in the area of quality assurance and control and therefore outside the scope of this book. However, quality requirements do have CM implications and these are dealt with.

(9) Handover: in the general case, a development ends with handover to a support group, or at least a change from a costly and risky development activitity to cheaper and less risky maintenance. If these benefits are to be achieved it is essential that the handover is carried out in a controlled fashion and further development is not allowed to masquerade as mainte-nance. It is, on the other hand, unlikely that development will cease completely on handover and some development support must be planned for and provided after this point.

(10) Internal documentation: while all admit that good internal documentation is essential to a successful product, in cases of shortage of time, money or people, documentation is the first thing to be cut. Careful advance planning can cause the generation of documentation simultaneously with the design and implementation of the system with only small overheads on the main process.

(11) Build strategy: for large products, adoption of a strategy of successive 'builds', whereby early versions of the software system with limited capability are produced well in advance of the final development, will greatly ease control problems.

(12) Maintenance and support procedures: many of the control procedures used during development are equally applicable to maintenance and support activities. For example, configuration identification methodology will not change after handover, while change control of code and documentation to deal with error corrections can use an identical methodology to that used in development. The testing process for corrected systems can also make

use of the same methods and tools as development testing, while major changes to operational systems will benefit from the use of baselines, reviews and a build strategy.

(13)   Software system 'production': if more than one copy of a software system is to be installed, more complex change control and archiving procedures are needed. In such a case we have an analogous situation to the production of hardware, and similar configuration controls are necessary. If the installations differ in any way there may be several versions of code to be handled

- actual installed systems, perhaps duplicated in an archive;
- the master system, the result of the development programme, which forms a basis for all the others and will be subsequently maintained and improved;
- the modifications to (a version of) the master system, which are used to generate the installed systems.

It is obvious that these interact in a complex fashion. For example, a change made to a master system to cure an error may invalidate one or more of the modifications and may produce incompatibilities with systems in the field. Thus, all such code must be changed only under control.

Not all of these areas warrant a separate procedure for any particular project, but the CM system adopted must take account of all the areas.

2.3 PROCEDURE PUBLICATION

If more than two people have an agreed procedure for doing anything, it is worth writing it down to avoid misunderstanding and disagreement. Indeed, even if only one person is involved, it is still often worth documenting — he will not have the job for ever. Most organisations involved in software development have a means of publishing such procedures or standard methods. Such publications can be used to document CM procedures. For small organisations or isolated production teams without such publication means, any formal or informal method of documenting procedures will suffice.

However, if the agreement of more than one department of an organisation is needed to operate a CM procedure, certain factors need to be stressed. First a method will be needed to publish draft versions of such a procedure and circulate them for approval by the interested parties. Once approval is obtained it is a useful psychological ploy, if nothing else, to get the representatives of the parties to sign something to indicate their approval. Procedures and their implications need to be fully understood if they are to operate correctly and the need to append one's signature to a document does much to concentrate the mind. Copies of agreed procedures must be made available to all relevant staff. This may mean an identification or reference number which transcends several departments.

Finally procedures may need to change with time, but in a controlled and agreed fashion.

The basic methodology for handling these matters can be similar to that used for publishing, agreeing and controlling baseline documents, which is described in chapter 5. The information needed to control such procedures can be contained in one standard front sheet. An example of such a sheet is shown in figure 2.3. It contains the following important information, indicated by circled note letters

- a unique reference number (a);
- a status box indicating if this is a proposal or an accepted and enforced procedure (b);
- a title (c);
- a distribution list (d);
- control information showing dates and issue numbers, authorisation levels and the author's name (e-j).

To aid in production and understanding of such procedures, it is recommended that the initial sections for every procedure should be standard and display such essential information as

- the purpose and scope of the procedure;
- the staff affected by the procedure;
- any relevant supporting documentation.

The sample procedures in the appendices use such standard sections.

We will leave this subject now, before it becomes too bureaucratic and frightens managers of simpler projects by its complexity. However, even this does make a point. In producing a book of this kind it is necessary to deal with the most complex situations: large projects, large teams, long timescales, multiple users, multiple sites, etc. In doing so, the methodology suggested may seem like overkill to the average project manager. He should not let himself be put off. Such a manager should merely regard the mechanisms described as a menu from which he can choose the courses which are applicable to his circumstances, and discard the rest.

2.4 PROJECT MANAGER'S CHECKLIST

Because of the wide variety of software development projects, it is not possible to specify exactly the CM procedures which must exist for any particular software system. It is, however, necessary to ensure that all those aspects of a particular system that need to be controlled are controlled. To help a project manager to discover all such areas, a questionnaire is provided as appendix A. This document, which should be read in conjunction with figure 2.2, focuses attention on the various aspects of project control in turn, in order to highlight areas where insufficient control exists. Because of the interaction of CM with other control systems, such as reporting mechanisms and quality assurance, these items are

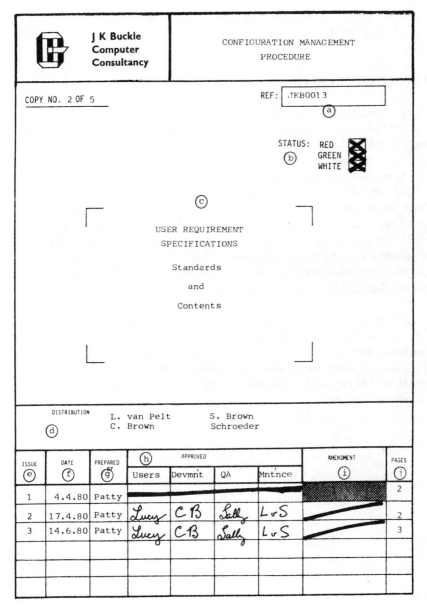

J K Buckle **Computer** **Consultancy**			CONFIGURATION MANAGEMENT PROCEDURE				

COPY NO. 2 OF 5   REF: JKB0013
ⓐ

STATUS: RED
ⓑ   GREEN
              WHITE

ⓒ

USER REQUIREMENT
SPECIFICATIONS

Standards

and

Contents

DISTRIBUTION   L. van Pelt   S. Brown
ⓓ   C. Brown   Schroeder

ISSUE ⓔ	DATE ⓕ	PREPARED BY ⓖ	ⓗ APPROVED				AMENDMENT ⓘ	PAGES ⓙ
			Users	Devmnt	QA	Mntnce		
1	4.4.80	Patty						2
2	17.4.80	Patty	*Lucy*	C B	*Sally*	L v S		2
3	14.6.80	Patty	*Lucy*	C B	*Sally*	L v S		3

Figure 2.3   A CM procedure

also covered in the checklist, as are the use of development tools and systems. The aim here is to draw attention to the need for interlocking controls and tools within any development.

Armed with this checklist, the list of possible CM procedures from the previous section, and a good deal of common sense, the project manager of a

project of any size should be able to define, establish and operate the CM
controls that his software needs.

2.5 CUSTOMISATION FOR PARTICULAR PROJECTS

This has already been dealt with in general terms in section 2.3. It is as
impossible to specify a generally applicable methodology for all software developments as it is to design a general-purpose factory, independent of the product.
Certainly organisations will differ and, even within organisations, some projects
may have different requirements from the rest.

IBM Federal Systems Division have managed to impose a very strict
development methodology with a strong CM basis. The results are impressive,
with three years of deliveries to time and within budget. However, the bureaucratic overheads of the system would be totally unrealistic for a normal DP
department. Even for organisations with a similar scale of problem, differences
in management style may make such a system inapplicable — IBM enjoy a level
of staff discipline that is the envy of other managers and the despair of other
staff!

In order to introduce CM techniques into a project or an organisation it is
necessary to adapt them. Essentially a project life-cycle model must be
developed, taking into account the current methods and tools. By mapping
this life-cycle on to that illustrated in figures 2.1 and 2.2, it will be possible to
isolate the CM mechanisms that are required and to consult the relevant
chapters of this book.

3 Baselines

One of the problems of working with software is that there are no natural, measurable entities that can be used to observe progress or quality between the initial conception and the final system. Indeed, even though the existence of a final system can be shown objectively, its quality or the way in which it meets or fails to meet the original requirements are difficult to demonstrate and, for any real system, impossible to prove conclusively.

A number of techniques have been built up over the years to help overcome this problem with software measurability. (See, for example, reference 2 for details of management techniques.) One of the most important of these is the concept of *baselines* or system milestones.

A baseline is a basis or reference point in the overall work schedule, whose achievement can be satisfactorily demonstrated. A baseline has three connected functions

- as a measurable progress point;
- as a basis for subsequent development and control;
- as a measurement point for assessing quality and fitness for purpose, before the final system is manifested.

To achieve these purposes, each baseline must mark a definite step in the progress from the initial statement of requirements for the system to the appearance of the deliverable software. It should therefore appear on the main line of activity between these points. For this reason, baselines normally take the form of the availability of ever more detailed descriptions of the system, at first in terms of documents and later in terms of actual software. Thus successive system baselines in a software development programme might be

- the statement of system requirements
- the total system specification } documents
- the detailed software specification
- the outline software design
- the detailed software design
  [internal module baselines]
- preliminary-system version
- first-release version } actual systems
- second-release version etc.

The entry in brackets is intended to show that, after the appearance of the

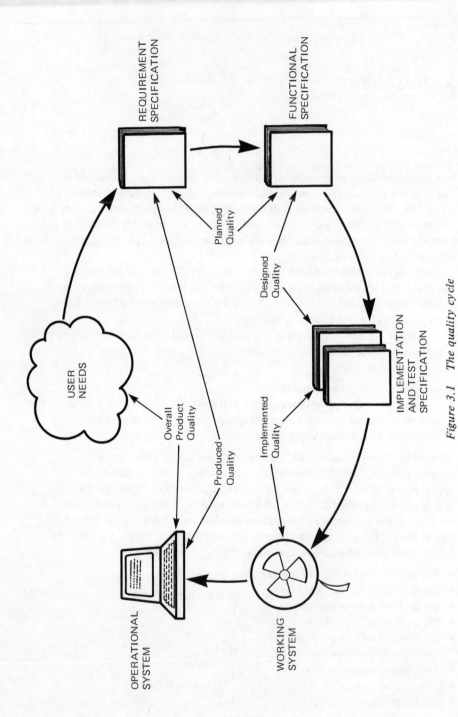

Figure 3.1   *The quality cycle*

detailed software design and before the preliminary system version is integrated, work will be concerned with individual modules and lower level module baselines may apply to these. Of course, for small projects some of these baselines could be collapsed, and for very large projects a particular baseline may appear in several steps.

In order that each baseline forms a firm platform on which to build, the end of each phase in the development programme and the start of the next is marked by the *acceptance* of a baseline. The form in which a baseline is accepted will vary in detail throughout the development phases but the criterion for acceptance will be the same in all cases: does the new baseline conform to the constraints imposed by previous baselines, and will the subsequent baselines and the final system it implies be achievable?

Thus the acceptance of the 'system specification' baseline will normally be by a design review of some sort that attempts to ensure that the requirements set out in the previous baseline are met and the methodologies and technologies implied are reasonable. The 'first release version' baseline on the other hand will be accepted by the successful completion of some validation tests that will have been based on the descriptions of the system contained in previous baselines. Figure 3.1 shows the sorts of quality measurement that can be made between various baseline points, using the basic development cycle of figure 1.1.

Acceptance of a baseline means that the document or code can be 'frozen' to form a solid foundation for the next stage of operations. However, since human activities are never perfect, there must always be the possibility that subsequent work or new requirements will show a need to modify a specification or change some software. A configuration management system must take account of such a possibility, but must ensure that the changes are made only after the same amount of investigation of the consequences, and with the same authority, that gave the original approval to the baseline. This gives rise to the concept of *change control* described in chapters 5 and 6.

3.1 BASELINES FOR SOFTWARE PROJECTS

Since the baseline represents the end achievement of each phase of development, the form of successive baselines can be deduced from the development schematic of figure 2.2. Each baseline should correspond to a major milestone in the development plan, and provision for involving the relevant internal and external authorities in the acceptance of each baseline must be built into the plan. Many of the mechanisms for doing this, such as design reviews, may already exist in software-development organisations. Others, such as inspections, are relatively new and are covered in more detail in a later chapter.

Figure 3.2 shows the development baselines adopted by TRW, a leader in the configuration-management field. TRW's systems are larger than most software projects but, since most other developments are subsets, we can use this diagram as a basis for discussion. This figure and the following two are taken

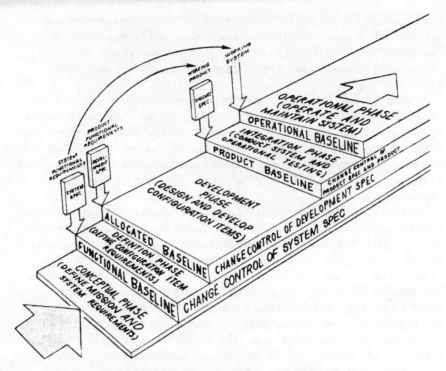

Figure 3.2   General system life-cycle model for baseline configuration management

from reference 1, and reproduced by kind permission of TRW. As the development of the system proceeds from left to right in the diagram, the achivement of each baseline is shown by a step. The primary phase of a TRW development is called the 'conceptual phase' and corresponds approximately to box 11 of figure 2.2. At the end of this phase, a system specification is produced, agreed and placed under change control. This represents the first or *functional baseline.* The terms used in this diagram stem from the military nature of TRW's systems.

Using the system specification as a controlled basis, the definition phase, corresponding approximately to boxes 12 and 13 of figure 2.2, generates a development specification. This document defines the functional requirements of the individual items that are to form the system. Agreement of the development specification constitutes the second or *allocated baseline.* The development specification is placed under change control and forms the start point for the development phase, in which the individual product components of the total system are designed in detail and implemented. This period corresponds approximately to boxes 21, 22 and 23.

The end result of the development phase is an actual working product plus a description of it contained in the product specification. These items now have to be agreed and accepted in order to constitute the third or *product baseline.*

The acceptance is based on the extent to which they do, or do not, meet the requirements set down in the development specification; this relationship is shown by the arrow joining them.

Once the product baseline has been achieved, the working product and its specification are placed under change control, signified by the next step up in the diagram. Note that at this stage, for the first time, actual code and data are being 'frozen' and subjected to change control, and not just documents. From this controlled baseline the integration phase proceeds; during this phase, system tests and operational tests are carried out. This corresponds to boxes 31 and 32 of figure 2.2. Successful completion of this testing means that the product, changed under control in response to the testing, becomes an operational working system. This point constitutes the final or *operational baseline* and means that a working system that conforms to the original system specification may be released. Note that no further level of change control is necessary here, since the items available at the product baseline have been transformed under change control to the releasable system. However, during the maintenance process, other complementary forms of control may be needed.

Figure 3.2 is, of course, a very simplified diagram, since it does not attempt to show the relationship between hardware and software development (necessary for systems like TRW's), the reviews and audits necessary, nor the more detailed control necessary during the development phase. Figure 3.3 adds these details. The basic phases, baselines and specification documents are unchanged from figure 3.2. The acquisition or development of hardware is shown as a parallel activity beginning at the functional baseline and coming back to join the software development after the product baseline has been achieved, so that system testing can take place. Figure 3.3 also shows a more detailed breakdown of the development phase. The development specification will have divided the software component of the total system into a number of independent software items (computer program configuration items or CPCIs, in TRW jargon). Two such items are shown in figure 3.3, although most developments would contain considerably more such separable components. For each CPCI there will be a preliminary design phase that will split the CPCIs down into smaller modules or routines, which will form units for coding purposes. The detailed design of each of these units is then performed, followed by their coding, debugging and checkout or unit test.

Up to this point the software-development process has been one of analysis – breaking down the total structure of the required system into manageable component parts which are then coded and checked out. After the checkout of the first few routines the process changes to one of synthesis – combining the individual items in order eventually to produce the total system. First, routines are built together to form CPCIs which can then be tested. At the end of the development testing of the software a preliminary master tape is formed and the system can then be validated. Validation, which will include acceptance tests, is normally carried out under the control of quality assurance staff other than the developers and, while the methodology may be similar, the emphasis is different.

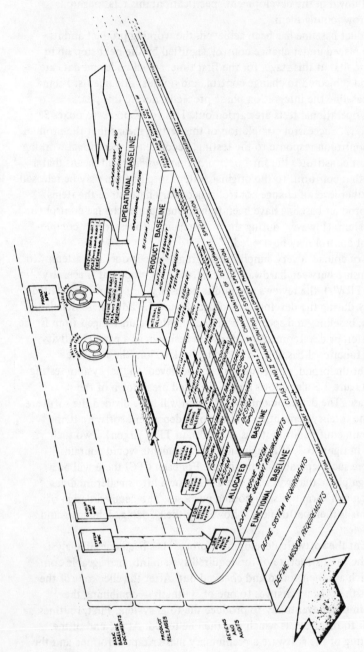

Figure 3.3   Detailed system life-cycle model for baseline configuration
management – 1

Development testing is designed to find errors that can be corrected. Validation, which does not begin until development testing is complete, is an attempt to prove, as far as possible, that no more errors remain.

Successful completion of the validation testing leads to the product baseline and the production of a master tape. The hardware and software paths then rejoin for system testing. Figure 3.3 also shows the position of major reviews and audits that are carried out throughout the development period. At least one is associated with the achievement of each baseline and in addition there are reviews associated with internal, lower level milestones.

The first major review is the system requirements review, which concentrates on the system specification that has been produced during the conceptual phase. This review is the mechanism for agreeing the system specification and thus inaugurating the functional baseline. A similar major review is carried out when the development specification is complete at the end of the definition phase, and here agreement leads to the allocated baseline.

Design reviews can be held at various points during the development phase, in particular when preliminary design and detailed design of individual CPCIs are complete. In addition, there will be lower level reviews at coding milestones within the project — these may often take the form of audits or code inspections. A further internal review of some form will also take place before the handover of the preliminary master tape for validation testing.

Major audits of the software from the point of view of quality, functions, fitness for purpose, issuability, produceability, etc., will also take place at the completion both of validation testing and system-operational testing. These audits or reviews, if successful, will lead to the product baseline and operational baseline, respectively. The classes of change control shown on the side of the steps are concerned with the authorities involved in approving the changes and need not concern us here.

Figure 3.3 is still not complete, in the sense that it does not show the documentation associated with the development process, apart from the three major baseline documents. Even for these no attempt is made to show the relationship between them, the various versions that are produced during the development cycle or the interactions between documents. Obviously certain documents apart from the major baseline documents need to be available at particular reviews; for example, an operator's manual is essential to realistic system testing.

The documentation standards adopted by TRW are added to the diagram in figure 3.4, which shows: the documents produced; the period over which they are each developed; and their relationship to each other, to product releases and to reviews. Since it is in details of the actual documentation required that standards are most likely to differ between TRW and other organisations, no detailed discussion of this figure is given here. Indeed, when reduced to the format of this book, the amount of information shown makes the diagram virtually unreadable in any case. Nevertheless, it would be instructive for a project manager to study the figure while drawing up his own project plan, in order to check both that the necessary documents were being produced and that they were being made

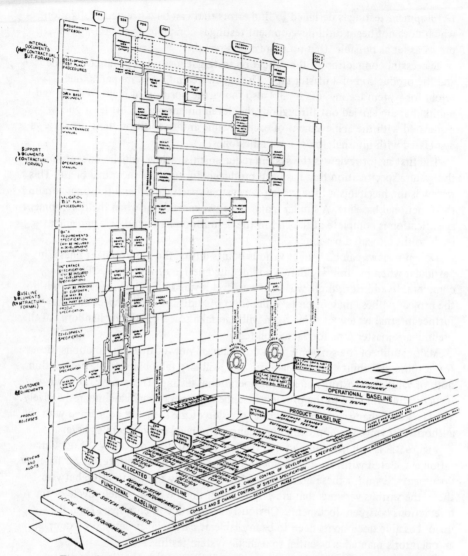

*Figure 3.4   Detailed system life-cycle model for baseline configuration
management – 2*

available at the right time. Some attention is devoted to development documents
in a later chapter.

3.2 ESTABLISHING DEVELOPMENT BASELINES

The discussion of section 3.1 provides a framework for the establishment of
specific CM baselines for software development. The development project

manager, in association with his management and any user committee or similar body, must determine what baselines are necessary for his project and incorporate the baseline achievements into his project plan. Whatever baselines are in fact chosen, each should conform to the following four criteria

- the baseline must be associated with the production of a physical item, either a document or a version of code;
- it is the *acceptance* of this item and not its initial appearance that constitutes the achievement of the baseline;
- acceptance is normally carried out by a review or audit of the item against requirements contained in previous baselines or, in the case of code, the successful completion of testing against previously specified criteria; achievement therefore represents a positive step towards system completion;
- once a baseline has been achieved, the item associated with it must be placed under formal change control.

The project manager should realise that there can be at least two levels of baseline. Project baselines will mark the end of each major phase of the project and will normally involve agreement by personnel outside the project. Usually, these will be representatives of the users or quality assurance staff, if the organisation supports this function separately. Changes to the baseline document or system version after this point will also involve the agreement of these external parties or their representatives. In addition to major baselines, there will be internal milestones, particularly during the development phase. These will normally involve only project staff. However, the rules for achieving the baseline and for placing the associated physical item under change control are identical in both cases.

The smaller the item associated with the baseline, the smaller the number of people that need to be associated with agreeing it and, later, agreeing changes to it. This is essential in order to ensure the short reaction time needed to correct problems encountered at a low level. Thus, while a change to the system specification is likely to have a major effect on the system, and must therefore be considered by all relevant parties at some length, changes to the code of a routine to correct an error found in validation is more localised and can be agreed, fairly quickly, between the programmer and a representative of the validation team, or the project manager or chief designer. Note, however, that even in the latter case formal change control is required, even if it operates in a simple, fast way. This ensures both that arbitrary changes are not made by an individual programmer without regard to the effects that these may have on other routines, and that the exact status of testing and acceptance of all system components is known at all times.

For each baseline incorporated into the project plan, therefore, the following information is required

- the name of the associated physical item which has to be agreed;
- the method to be adopted for agreement (review, audit, inspection, etc.);

Table 3.1 Development baseline definitions

Baseline	Associated item	Agreement method	Approval authorities	Associated documentation
1 Functional	System specification	Review	Steering committee	Statement of system requirements
2 Allocated	Software specification	Review	Steering committee	System specification; preliminary design documents; test and validation requirements
2a Preliminary design	Software design specifications	Review/audits	Design review members	Software specification; preliminary product specifications
2b Critical design	Detailed design documents	Audits/inspections	Internal staff/design review members	Software design specifications; preliminary product specifications; validation plan; preliminary user documents
2c Unit milestone	Software units	Inspections or audits of testing	Internal staff	Test plans; test results; detailed design documents
3 Product	Software system	Review of validation	Steering committee	Validation plans; validation results; user documentation; final product specifications

- the approval authorities, that is, the people responsible both for agreeing the item and for approving subsequent changes to it;
- the associated documentation required to permit adequate review.

While, as stressed above, the baselines will vary from project to project, consideration of figure 2.2 suggests the contents of table 3.1 as a starting point for consideration by the project manager. The 'approval authorities' column is meant only to give an indication of the level of approval needed.

In practice, there may be several baselines corresponding to 2c to approve individual unit coding, check-out and integration testing. Again, in many projects it is possible (and advisable) to produce a number of separate 'builds' of the product, with increasing levels of facilities and performance (see section 12.2). The achievement of these internal builds would introduce other baselines between 2c and 3. These would be of similar form to the final product baseline, but may involve a lower level of approval.

A simple description of the documentary baselines needed for a medium-sized project is given in the procedure of appendix B.3.

3.3 SPECIFICATION FORMATS AND STANDARDS

It will be seen from section 3.2 that most of the baselines for software development take the form of specifications, ranging from the initial requirements, which is a system specification in user terms, through to the software engineer's workbooks, which contain detailed specifications in technical terms of the pieces of software that make up the system. For control and auditing purposes, all such documents must contain information to show at least their author, the date and/or issue number and the level of approval that they have received. After initial approval they must also carry a change control record to enable configuration status accounting to be carried out.

The minimum standardisation of such specifications needed is that they should each carry a sheet with this control information contained in it. In practice, further standardisation of internal documents is usually worthwhile, since it means that common information will be placed in a standard position within the document and presented in a standard way. Again, it is worthwhile to standardise on the levels of approval needed, in order to remove ambiguity. The procedure of appendix B.1 provides a method for standardising the relevant specification baselines for a system and displaying the standard accounting procedure on a single front sheet. It is consistent with the document status and change control methods defined in chapter 5. An example of the use of such a front sheet is shown in figure 5.1 while figure 5.2 shows a page from an actual baseline document.

3.4 APPLICATION TO SMALLER PROJECTS

The idea of baselines is equally applicable to a one-man project or a hundred-man project and the advantages to be gained are similar. The differences come in the formality needed, the people involved in agreement and control and the actual form of the baselines.

Paradoxically, the smaller the project the more difficult it often is to get the initial requirements specified and agreed. In the average DP department this can lead to high costs either in development or in maintenance, as misunderstandings in real user requirements are put right. The aim for the manager of such a project should be to get as complete a statement as possible of a new development and, even if a formal signed document is not appropriate, to indicate that development will proceed on that basis. Change control is essential in such circumstances since newly discovered requirements will have to be balanced against increases in cost and/or timescales, or reductions in performance. In such circumstances analysis and design methods which allow feedback to the potential user are invaluable. These enable a user to understand what is being done, to participate in the specification process, and to compare the result with his requirement. For examples of such methods see references 4 to 6.

With later baseline items, the only difference between large and small projects will be the size of the specification documents and the testing and validation required. With the same staff responsible for both producing and testing code there is an even more rigorous requirement for well-defined test plans that are strictly adhered to. It may well be possible to combine many of the items of table 3.1 into single documents, but these should reflect each of the aspects separately. For example, confusion between functional requirements and design are a common cause of unsatisfactory software systems.

The development of an individual life-cycle model, as suggested in the preceding chapter, will determine *where* the baselines should be and provide a basis for the definition of *what* they should contain.

4 *Configuration Identification*

No control of any sort is possible for a software system unless the system, the versions of the system and its component parts can be uniquely identified. This is not just a bureaucratic, administrative problem; consider the problem of finding an error in a system if several versions exist and it is not known which has exhibited the error.

Configuration identification provides the means to isolate the components that make up a system, as a basis for control. There are three dimensions to this: first, the system must be broken down into a number of known, manageable parts; second, these parts must be uniquely named; last, as these parts change with time, the various versions that appear must also be uniquely identified. The first dimension is closely bound up with the processes of specification, analysis and design. The other two require rigorously enforced standards.

It is obviously necessary that any complete system shall have a unique identification and, in addition, it must be possible to distinguish between any versions of the system that may exist. Such versions may have been steps towards a final version, or customised alternatives, available on different sites or to different users. While this is all that is logically necessary, it is useful that, where a system is composed of modules, these in turn have identifiers and version numbers. This is particularly true where any of these modules are 'library' modules, that is, items of program or data that may be used in other systems and are possibly produced by other development units. Again, even the naming and numbering of the whole system and its atomic parts may be insufficient from a practical viewpoint. 'Molecular' subsystems may also need a name and a version.

A less obvious problem is the fact that a software CM item (that is, a unit of software to which CM techniques can be applied) may exist in many forms, and each form may be stored or exist on several different media. For example, a subroutine may be in source, compiled-relocatable or compiled-absolute forms. Indeed, we may even consider documentation such as a functional specification or user guide to be a 'form' of the software item. If we do not, we must have a separate identification system for such documentation and a means of relating versions to appropriate systems. Again, a particular form, such as a source program, may exist as a listing, a paper tape, card or magnetic file. Each of these forms must be identifiable and the same form on different media must be recognisable. These matters are easily dealt with by adopting almost any simple naming standard and indeed, the matter has normally been given some thought in most software development environments.

An even less obvious problem, which is not in general solved in many organisations, occurs with compiled, runnable systems. These may exist as files on several media, and such files can be labelled with the appropriate identification. However, they can also exist as actual operational programs in a computer store or as a dump. In these latter forms the label information has been lost, but when several versions are available it is obviously useful, if not essential, that a post-mortem dump should identify uniquely the program that it represents.

These, then, are the sort of considerations that give rise to the configuration identification standards dealt with in the following sections. We look here at the most complicated forms of naming systems. Simple projects may well need only a subset of the standards described. However, before deciding on any standards to be used in a particular project it is wise to consider the full requirements over the whole life-cycle of the system. Adopting a system that suffices for the initial development but cannot cope with multiple installations, for example, is a false economy.

The preface warned that some sections of the book would be less than enthralling; the rest of this chapter tends to be downright boring. It is recommended for detailed reading only when a new identification system is being established or an old one assessed for completeness.

4.1 ESTABLISHING CONTROL UNITS

Figure 3.4 showed how, at the end of the system definition phase, the development specification described a number of individual computer program configuration items or CPCIs, which were used as the basis for the development phase. These items were then subdivided further during the design process, eventually reaching the module or routine level, which forms a unit for coding or for inclusion from an existing library.

Since each of the items at each of the levels may be manipulated, amended or replaced as an entity, each needs a unique name. Whether this name is the one by which the unit is known to the compiler or linker that operates on it, or is a separate name, will depend entirely on the tools being used in the development project. It would obviously be easier if, for example, the unit name of a module for configuration management purposes were the same as its source language name, but language limitations may make this difficult if not impossible. Again, while controllable items may have a random, unique name with a list being maintained to ensure uniqueness, the system is much more manageable if names are in fact hierarchical. This is obviously simpler to implement if a top-down design methodology is used.

The full name of a compilable unit might then be of the form

project . program . subsystem . unit

Providing we store the items themselves in a hierarchical fashion (or alternatively maintain separately the tree structure that determines the position of the unit within the overall system), we can then refer to the item locally merely by its unit name. The context in such a case is clear, and the item will not be confused with other units of the same local name in other subsystems or programs. Common units or subsystems can be treated in the same way. Alternatively, we can identify an item by its mathematical position in the hierarchy, for example $S_{1,2,3}$ for unit 3 of subsystem 2 of program 1.

The form of organisation implied by such systems cries out for automation, and there are in fact several tools available to help with the complexity of managing large systems of this nature. More will be said of this below and in chapter 11.

Whatever system is used, we must assume for control purposes that each item and each item collection of the system can be uniquely identified by name. This provides a static decomposition of the system. We next require a means of distinguishing different versions as they change with time.

4.2 VERSIONS, FORMS AND MEDIA

Versions of controllable items may be identified by appending to the name a number or other set of characters that identify the version.

Different versions may arise during development as facilities are added, or after initial development as enhancements are added. Such major changes are normally termed 'builds' or 'releases'. For any particular release of a CM item, a number of versions may be made for different installations or to correct errors before the next release. Thus a version identifier might take the form

> *release number . version*
> for example, 3.27 for version 27 of release 3; or 3.HH for a version
> of release 3, customised for a system designated by HH

A further subfield may be necessary if temporary patches are made to particular versions: for example, 3.HH.C1-3 would means version 3.HH with corrections numbered 1 to 3 applied. Such corrections would need to be documented in some well-defined place.

Such version identifiers apply to code items. A document may also have its own issue numbers that do not correspond directly to releases or corrections of the corresponding software, and these must be clearly indicated for control purposes. Alternatively, a date may be used to give such information.

Note that not all forms of a CM item may use all the fields of the version identifier. For example, if versions for a particular installation are generated by invoking compile-time features such as conditional compilation or macros, an item in source form would only have a release number, while an item in loadable form could have a version number as well.

Individual items may also appear in several *forms.* For simple CM items the most obvious forms are source and relocatable code, apart from various associated documents. Composite items may have other associated 'forms'; for example, the linkage parameters for a particular system, or the operational JCL are important CM items and need to be controlled in the same way as the actual code. The overall item identification should allow the form to be distinguished where applicable.

The final difference is the medium on which the item exists — paper tape, disc file, readable document, etc. This part of the name is obviously only needed for reference from elsewhere, for example, the index to an archive, but again the total item identification sequence should take this requirement into account.

Such a total item identification appears extremely complex, but each of the parts is needed to reference an item uniquely, particularly if it is archived or otherwise stored, and all CM items must contain or display their name if they are to be uniquely identified.

4.3 ITEM LABELLING

As stated above, every configuration-management item must declare its full name to allow it to be uniquely identified. For such purposes as archiving, this name should appear in a standard place and a standard format. For example, an archived item on paper tape should have some form of label showing

item identifier . version identifier . form identifier

and indexes to any archive should contain the same information, plus a medium identifier. In other circumstances, while most, if not all, the information is necessary, it may be presented less formally. Three cases must be considered and are dealt with separately below:

Documents

Items such as system specifications or user guides are CM items that are intended to be read only by humans — although they may exist as part of a machine file at times and are then subject to the considerations regarding physical items detailed below. Apart from the medium, which is self-evident, all the items of the name are required, but may be presented in the most convenient form for human readership. Figure 5.1, for example, allows all the relevant information to be provided by the combination of a reference number, a title and an issue/amendment number. Note that, although this document corresponds to a particular software system, neither its issue number nor necessarily its component parts have a direct correspondence to releases or components of that system. This matter will be dealt with in more detail later.

Physical Items

Physical items such as tapes or floppy discs that contain machine-readable items subject to configuration management will also need to be identified by humans. Such items should therefore be labelled to give the name of the item held and possibly other archival information. Even in small projects this is much safer than the usual initials and date found on data items lying in the corners of programmers' drawers. To avoid the disasters that this may cause the overhead is small.

Machine-readable Items

Labelling a physical item is not in itself sufficient since the contents of such an item may be read by a machine and used to generate other items that will not be automatically labelled. Machine-readable items should thus contain an indication of their name in machine-readable form. As far as source language items are concerned, a combination of the choice of module name and use of a TITLE directive or its equivalent or, failing that, comments allows the programmer to incorporate the complete CM name into the source and this should be made a standard for all projects.

How to store the same information into compiled code is a less easily soluble problem. It is very important, however, since without it a dump can never be associated with the relevant source with certainty — a vital need when dealing with problems in delivered systems. The method adopted by many large software companies is to include the name as a character-string constant that will appear at a standard place in any dump. Normally this is only done at the system level for delivered systems, since the name and version numbers of individual components can be traced from that point. However, during development a similar standard for all components is sometimes useful. The way in which the name is stored and accessed will depend on the source language used. One company known to the author that uses Fortran heavily stores the name in a common block and accesses the first word of it as the first statement of the master program in order to pinpoint its location. Another large software house using a system that allows multiple program-entry points reserves one of them for a sequence of instructions that will print out the full name information. Unless some major corruption has occurred, this entry is invoked as part of any dump procedure. Bell Laboratories, in their SCCS system, [7] have a provision for entering version numbers automatically into modules in various source languages to achieve the same effect, and other commercially available systems provide similar facilities. Whatever system is adopted as being most convenient, all projects should ensure that the complete name information appears in the actual object code of complete systems as a very minimum.

4.4 REGISTRATION

If we consider both the temporary versions of CM items that appear during development and the need to correct errors found, we arrive at a position where several differing versions of a particular item may exist and be in use at one time. While the naming conventions outlined above will distinguish between such versions, they will not say in what way the versions differ, nor indeed why different versions exist. This can only be done by *registration,* that is, maintaining an index of versions and of items with details of each. Such registers are useful for other purposes as well. For example, registers of low level CM objects provide a library index to allow others to use directly, or adapt, existing modules and subsystems rather than redevelop from scratch.

The ideal way of maintaining such registers, if suitable tools are available, is to store the relevant information in, or associated with, the source code of the version, and to have a means of extracting and displaying the information when necessary. SCCS [7] and its derivatives [8] provide this sort of facility in conjunction with naming control, as do several available library handlers. This matter is, of course, closely connected with code change control, which is dealt with in more detail in a later chapter.

Particularly when CM units pass outside the control of the authors (that is, developed units go to maintenance or validated systems are handed over to operations), a further aspect of registration occurs. Errors will undoubtedly be found and must be recorded and corrected. If the corrections take the form of temporary patches, these must be recorded and steps taken to replace them by clean compilations as soon as convenient, to ease maintenance costs. Such information can be considered as additions to the basic registration file and easily handled, provided the need is taken into account from the start. Again these matters are considered in more detail in later chapters.

Finally, a third aspect of registration is needed to deal with a problem mentioned in section 4.3. A specification document and a section of code may be thought of as different forms of the same item. Changes to each of these may proceed independently. For example, a new issue of a document may be needed to make some element of the description clearer and will have no effect on the corresponding code. Conversely, a better algorithm or data layout may be applied to a section of code, producing a new version, but both old and new will be equally well described by the same functional specification. However, some changes will be interrelated. A change to a requirements document will normally cause corresponding changes in code, while correction of an error in code may need corresponding changes in the design documents and user manuals. Such interaction is taken into account in the procedures specified for document and code change control in chapters 5 and 6. However, it is still necessary to retain details of what particular code versions correspond to which documents, and this again is a matter for registration. A similar but more easily understood problem exists with recording which versions of low level CM items are contained in particular versions of higher level subsystems or systems.

Registration, then, in its entirety, is a matter of keeping cross-references between all items under CM control to show their interactions, interrelationships and usage. It is not necessary to maintain large volumes of paper to record such interactions, however, or even computer files carrying the electromagnetic equivalents of the paper. A much more appropriate approach is that individual CM items should carry with them the requisite information, which can be extracted and displayed when necessary. Whether this is in fact possible depends on the tools used; this is discussed in a later chapter.

4.5 PRACTICAL APPLICATION OF CI

With small teams and small amounts of code being produced, the need for formality in identification methods is reduced. Nevertheless, the need to identify items, versions of items and corresponding documentation uniquely is as great for small teams as for large. The overhead of operating a standard naming and registration system is so small, and the cost of a lost or mixed version of a component so large, that it is worthwhile considering standards for item naming and registration even on one-person projects. With a smaller number of items to be controlled, the form of identification can, of course, be simpler but it should still be possible to identify any system component exactly.

The real trick for configuration identification is the use of sensible computer-based tools. This subject has already been mentioned and is expanded in chapter 11. The use of a tree-structured file-store for components can mean that the name of the component is its file-store location. With this as a basis, we can add SCCS-like tools to control versions of items. We can structure the file-store so that commonly available items are distinguishable from private, unvalidated development versions. We can use tools (see, for example, references 13 and 15) to keep track of the interactions between components and to ensure that the right versions of components are used in the construction of a system. We can even tackle the inevitable problems of co-ordination of changes in widely used library modules — a major problem in large projects — by letting the system keep track of what is changed and what effects this might have. Configuration identification is necessary but boring, which is an exact description of a task that should be solved by computer.

5 Document Production and Document Change Control

One of the basic foundations of configuration management is *configuration control.* By this process, changes to established baselines are classified, evaluated, approved or disapproved, released, implemented and verified. The prime purpose of configuration control is to ensure that the definition or configuration of the program used in critical phases of implementation, testing, acceptance and delivery is known and is compatible with the specification. It also ensures that, when changes are proposed to an agreed baseline, the same degree of consideration and the same acceptance criteria as for the initial baseline are applied. This is to prevent the unwitting application of what appears to be a minor change by local considerations, which turns out to have a major, unforeseen effect on other areas. This basic concern is similar regardless of whether the change is an alteration to a program specification or a patch to a stable program version.

Closely connected with configuration control is the idea of *configuration status accounting.* This is the process of recording, and reporting to interested parties, all information concerning the status of various baselines concerned with a software system, proposed changes to baselines and the implementation status of approved changes. Again this information is equally important for documents that constitute baselines and for actual code. However, although the necessity for control and accounting is similar for documents and code, the methodology must differ in each case because of the essentially different nature of these items. This chapter is concerned with a methodology for controlling documents: code change control is dealt with in the next chapter.

There are obviously two connected processes concerned with the establishment of a control system for baseline or prime specification documents: first, to produce such a document and have it approved; second, to deal with subsequent changes proposed to it. Each of these are dealt with in the following sections. The documents that are to be covered by this control mechanism should be standard within a development group, or agreed early in a particular development program. Their production should be incorporated into the development plan. These matters were dealt with in detail in chapter 3. In particular, there must be a list of such documents available to all relevant staff. The format of any individual document is not relevant to the control procedures provided that there is provision for clearly displaying at least

- a unique name and/or reference;
- the author's name;
- the date and/or issue number to distinguish this version from any subsequent version;
- the level of approval received to distinguish accepted documents from proposals;
- a status accounting record.

As explained in chapter 3, this can best be provided by a single standard front sheet, and the form of such a sheet is defined in appendix B.1. The following sections assume that this or some equivalent format is used for specification documents. An example of such a front sheet is shown in figure 5.1 and is used for definition purposes in subsequent sections; the circled numbers refer to key features of the document

- the unique reference of the document (1);
- the name of the project or system (2); this can actually be discovered from the reference but is a useful, if redundant, piece of information for a human reader;
- the change control status of the document (3);
- the title, and possibly a list of contents (4);
- the distribution list (5);
- issue details (6)-(11); the last line refers to this issue of the document; previous entries provide a historical record — in particular, the signatures of the approval authorities (9).

It can be seen that all the requirements mentioned above are included on this sheet, including status accounting information.

Standardisation of contents or layout is much more difficult. Figure 5.2 shows an example of an internal page that itself contains control information at the top. Whether this, and such items as standard sections, are also useful depends very much on the environment.

The remainder of this chapter is concerned with the production of specification documents such as these and the change control procedures that can be applied to them.

5.1 DOCUMENT REFERENCES AND STATUS

Since the variety of documents that may be placed under change control is very wide, no attempt is made here to propose a standard for references. Indeed, in some projects, a numbering system for externally available documents may be imposed by the contract or by internal organisation standards. However, there are some requirements that need to be covered in any numbering scheme.

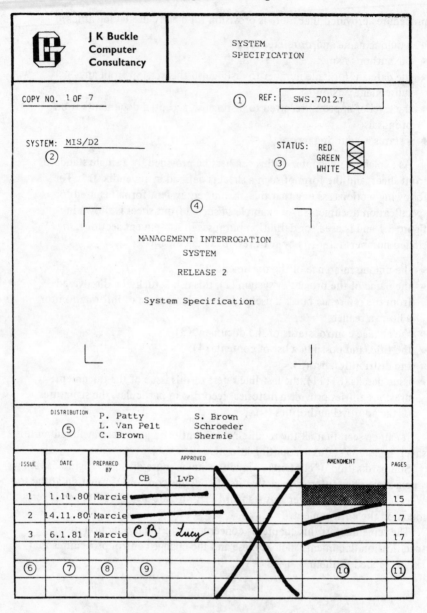

Figure 5.1   Example of a specification document

Certainly the number must be unique. In the absence of an organisation-wide scheme, this means in practice that the reference must contain an indication of the project/product or of the development involved. When several versions of a document are produced, they will have the same reference but be distinguished by an issue number.

MANAGEMENT INTERROGATION SYSTEM	SWS.701 23	
Release 2 System Specification	Page 1	of 17
	Edition 3	Date 5.1.81

0   CONTENTS

    1   Scope

    2   Document History

    3   Referenced Documents

    4   System Functional Specification

    5   Detailed user interface

    6   Boundary conditions and constraints

    7   Quality and reliability considerations

    8   Standards to be employed

    Appendix: Outline System Design Model

1   SCOPE

This document describes the second version of the Management Interrogation System (MIS/D) in terms of the software functions, gross level descriptions of the components and the use of hardware. It thus forms the basis for all software and associated development. In particular it contains the rules for determining:

–   the detailed software design

–   the use of hardware facilities

–   testing and validation to be covered

–   user manuals and education.

The system described meets all the requirements stated in Reference 1.

2   DOCUMENT HISTORY

2.1   Changes from previous version

Minor amendments to Section 6. First RED version.

2.2   Changes Forecast

None.

3   REFERENCES

    1   User requirements for new Interrogation system URS.701/2

    2   System Specification for Management Interrogation System SWS.6317F/5

    3   Use of test tools in the DP Department CMP3/2

4   SYSTEM FUNCTIONAL SPECIFICATION

From a functional point of view the system differs little from the previous release (Reference 2), the main changes

Figure 5.2   Sample specification page

The other important characteristic of a document is its status. Before a document is agreed, a draft version will have to be produced for the approval

authorities to study. It is important that the draft and approved versions be
clearly distinguished, since readers may only depend on agreed versions as a
basis for further work. Thus in a development project a programmer may start to
do detailed unit design before the system design document is approved. He must
know, however, that only an approved design document can form a stable basis
for his work and, while he can certainly use an unapproved document if no
approved one is available, he must do so with caution.

There is thus the need for distinguishing at least two classes of documents:
approved and unapproved. In practice a third category is often helpful. An author
may wish to produce an early draft of a document, not necessarily complete in
all details, for comment. Such documents are obviously a very insecure basis for
subsequent work. After one or more such drafts he will eventually produce a
version with which he is satisfied and which he is prepared to submit to the
approval process. Such documents are much more secure than the early drafts,
but still not 'frozen' in the sense that an approved document will be. We thus
have three broad categories of status

- initial proposals, not necessarily completely thought out, published for
  discussion and comment;
- firm proposals made by the author and capable of being submitted for
  approval;
- approved 'frozen' documents, subject to rigorous control of changes.

Note that only the final category is subject to formal change control and both
the former types can be changed unilaterally by the author. Further subcategories
are possible, but in practice these three are normally found to be sufficient. We
require a short name for each of these status categories. Such names must be
'neutral', in the sense that they should not imply specific methods of moving
from one status category to another, since the actual proposal and approval
methods will vary from project to project. Use of terminology already common
in other areas, such as 'working', 'draft', 'final', etc., may not be appropriate, or
may be misinterpreted. Instead this book applies a simple colour name to each
of the categories defined above

- initial proposals are *white;*
- firm proposals are *green;*
- approved documents are *red.*

These names are totally arbitrary and the reader can substitute others as he thinks
fit.

The status should be clearly shown on the front of any specification. In figure
5.1, this is done by the status box (3). The box applying to the appropriate status
is checked. If the status of a document changes, for example a green document is
approved, the new box can be checked without changing the rest of the cover
sheet.

5.2 PRODUCING SPECIFICATION DOCUMENTS

There are three classes of people associated with any document that is to be placed under change control

- *the originator:* that is, the author of the document; if the document is in fact produced by several persons, one must be made responsible for its completion and maintenance;
- *the approval authorities* : these are the people who must agree the document in order for the corresponding baseline to be accepted, and who will later need to approve changes;
- *readers* : these are the remainder of the people who use the document in order to carry out their own tasks.

An SADT diagram showing the relationship of these three classes, and the need for a procedure to resolve disagreements between them, is shown in figure 5.3. Essentially, the document originator produces proposals in the form of white or green status documents and circulates them to the approval authorities and the reader list. Comments from these parties will cause him to produce further versions until agreement is reached or a deadlock exists. Note that responses from approval authorities act as a control on these operations (that is, they must be taken into account), while the views of readers, which go to both the author and the approval authorities, are treated as input and may be ignored if necessary. In the case of a deadlock a resolution meeting is held and a final decision taken.

    Once the document is agreed, the signatures of the approval authorities are obtained and the specification becomes of red status and subject to change control. A flowchart of the actions of the originator is shown in figure 5.4. Note the initial emphasis on establishing contacts. While the signing-off of the document is a formal operation, it is best that all preceding operations be carried out in as informal a manner as possible, with the maximum of personal contact. Merely sending green specifications to approval authorities without warning or explanation is unlikely to be an efficient way of proceeding. All interested parties should be kept informed of progress, problems and decisions and the aim of the originator should be to maintain sufficient contacts to ensure that the signing-off process to approve the document is a mere formality. This can only be achieved if he is aware of the views of each of the approval authorities, at least in outline, before the final green version is published.

    The procedure of appendix B.2 describes in more detail the steps concerned in producing documents for placing under change control. The process can be applied not only to major specifications that constitute baseline achievement, but also to internal documents where more than one person is vitally concerned with the content. In the latter case, the change-authorities list will be very small and the procedure can be operated in a very fast and informal manner. Nevertheless, the standard front sheet and a formal sign-off is recommended even in such cases.

    The process of producing and agreeing documents and placing them under

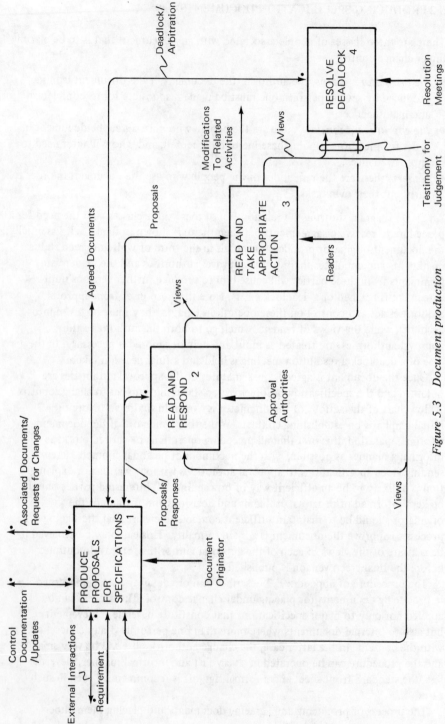

Figure 5.3   Document production

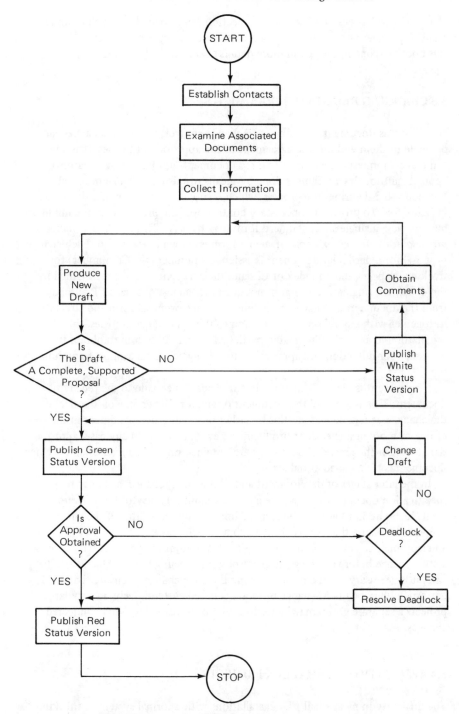

Figure 5.4 Producing documents for change control

change control as described in the next section can also apply to such items as plans, timescales and resource requirements. Such usage is outside the scope of this book; anyone interested in more details should consult reference 2.

5.3 CHANGING RED STATUS DOCUMENTS

All red status documents are subject to change control; that is, no changes can be made to them without the agreement of the approval authorities. Anyone can make a request for a change to a red document, not just the originator or approval authorities, and this is done by means of raising a change proposal. Procedure B.2 describes the process, which is shown in the form of a flowchart in figure 5.5. To provide the necessary control over the process with the minimum bureaucracy, a single-sheet standard form may be used. This is called a *change proposal form* and an example of such a form is shown in figure 5.6. Each change proposal for a particular document is assigned a number (the CP number) for tracking purposes and an index of CPs and their current status is maintained by the document originator. The person requiring a change obtains a CP number from the document originator, completes a change proposal form and circulates it, together with any relevant information to the approval authorities, the originator and any other interested parties. It is then up to him to obtain the necessary consideration and approval of the change or, if he cannot, to withdraw the CP.

   If agreement is reached, an amendment needs to be made to the red status document. This is done by the document originator. Depending on the size of the change needed, he may do this by either producing an amendment in the form of one or more new sheets, or producing a new document. In any case, approval signatures for the amended document are obtained on the front sheet and the new document is then issued at red status.

   In the later stages of development and during maintenance, a change to a specification document will require a corresponding change to the software itself. It should normally be the responsibility of the originator of the change proposal to ensure that this is done. In some urgent cases, for example, when an error must be corrected in an operational system, it may be necessary to make a code change before agreeing the corresponding documentation change. In this case, it is necessary for the person making the code change to ensure that a corresponding document change proposal is raised. Alternatively, in very large projects a separate group may be responsible for following up such connected changes.

5.4 APPLICATION TO SMALLER PROJECTS

The difficulty in most small EDP installations with a formal system of this kind is not the standardisation of document covers or references, which impose little

RESPONSIBILITY

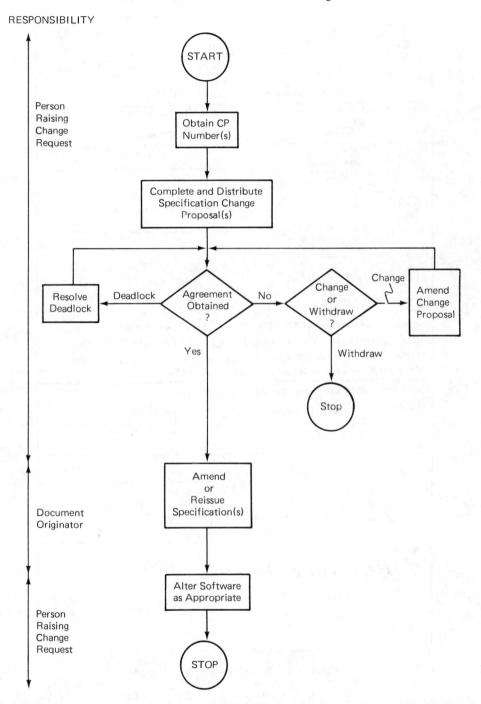

Figure 5.5   Document change procedure

DOCUMENT			CP number: **2**
	CHANGE PROPOSAL		

Document Reference: **SWS. 7012 J**	Edition **3**	Date **7.2.81**

Change Raised by: **Woodstock**	Project: **MIS/D2**

Other Affected Documents: **None**	Other Affected Projects: **None**

Reason for Change: Reference

☐ Corrections to system
  Change already made?
  ☐ Yes   ☐ No   _____

☑ Specification Error   Memo Franklin to C.B. 1.2.81

☐ Improvement request
  Finance or timescales affected
  ☐ Yes   ☐ No   _____

☐ Other (give details)

Description of Change (attach further pages if necessary):

Before attempting to use the 'DISPLAY IMPACT' function
the user must have previously 'SCAN'ned to the
area head. This requires changes to the state table
and operation nesting. Details attached.

Consequences of Change (attach further pages if necessary):

Localized and covered by new plans.

Tick if change is outside limits of approval authorities.   ☐ Yes

Approval Authorities:	Further Distribution:
C. Brown	S. Brown Franklin
L. van Pelt	Schroeder
	Shermie
	Marcie

Comments:

New tests needed.

Figure 5.6   Sample change proposal sheet

overhead, but with obtaining co-operation in operating a change proposal and
approval system. Managers of small DP departments, for example, often find it

very difficult to force their users to be precise or to commit themselves to paper. In such circumstances, while an attempt should be made to involve the users at least in approval and maintenance of the early specification documents, if such attempts fail all is not necessarily lost. Benefits can still be obtained by operating the system within the DP team, and there will be less overhead involved in terms of meetings, etc. Documents should still be circulated to user representatives and the process can at least be used to pinpoint the cost of late specification changes or forgotten facilities. In time, the users may even be persuaded that it is to their advantage to make up their minds early and to join in with the approval and change cycle. If not, even a totally internal change and control system will make the project manager's tasks somewhat easier.

6 *Code Change Control*

If it is important to produce and agree documents in an orderly manner and then change them only under control, it is of even more importance that the actual code which forms a product should be treated in the same way. Equally vital is the need for corresponding changes in code and documentation to be kept in step.

As far as development units are concerned, there are two periods that require rather different treatment: the actual development period before any software is finally integrated into a system; and system validation and the period following release of the first version, when there are one or more actual users whose needs must also be considered. For each of these periods there is another binary split between changes to code that correspond to changes to specifications and therefore involve a document change, on the one hand, and changes that do not affect specification documentation (for example, reprogramming of small sequences of code to give better performance), on the other. The former are automatically more visible, and special attention has to be devoted to the latter to avoid the confusion caused by seemingly identical versions of software that in practice exhibit different qualities.

The release period will eventually merge into a maintenance activity, where again two types of changes may arise. Planned enhancements will give rise to changes to code that are similar to the development period, while error corrections require their own control processes. Finally, if, instead of being a single installation software system, the product of development is delivered to more than one site or sold to more than one customer, there appears a genuine element of production, which may give rise to changes for particular installations only. Each of these forms of change is dealt with in subsequent sections.

6.1 SPECIFICATION CHANGES

Changes in specification with corresponding code changes may arise externally or internally. External changes normally occur because of changed requirements and are dealt with by normal document change control procedures. However, if code has already been written and will need to be modified to meet the new specification, not only must this be taken into account when considering the change but, if the change is approved, there must be a method of ensuring that the code changes accordingly. The 'comments' section of the change proposal form illustrated in figure 5.6 can be used to record such changes and set the necessary work in train. With most developments this may be all that is required. With larger, more complex projects this may need to be supplemented by a more formal system, recording in detail the changes required and scheduling the work necessary.

Internal specification changes arise when, during coding, errors or inadequacies are discovered in earlier, documentary baselines. It is therefore necessary to change the specification to conform to the code actually produced. This is easier to handle and is already taken care of by the documentation change proposal system.

6.2   INTERNAL SOFTWARE CHANGES

Until a software unit or module has been released by its originator for use by another person, any changes made to it, provided they continue to meet the specification, can be completely under the originator's control. Even when the software has been given to other people — for example, to allow them to test inter- faces — the originator can still change the items as he wishes, but he must of course tell his users what he is doing. In either of these cases it is essential that the origin- ator keeps careful track of the changes he is making and the various versions he produces.

Apart from a rigid system of version numbers (which are included in the code), as described in chapter 4, no formal systems are required for this purpose. How- ever, the use of an archive system, as outlined in chapter 4 and dealt with in more detail in chapter 11, can automate the tracking process and keep things in order. It is also in the programmer's own interest to keep records of changes made and reasons, and again these can be stored in the archive along with the new code, or recorded separately as part of the programmer's internal documentation.

Only when the originator hands over a version of his code for integration into a system that forms a product baseline does he lose his right to change it. He may, of course, produce new versions for his own purposes, but he should not be able to change the actual units he has handed over without approval of the other parties affected.

6.3   BASELINE CHANGES

The acceptance of sections of code for incorporation into a system effectively places them under change control of the same sort as that placed on specification baselines. If changes are made to any element of code — to correct errors found by validation, for example — it will be necessary to ensure that these changes are compatible with the rest of the system and do not introduce new errors. Essentially, a change authority is needed for the system baseline and it is the function of this authority to approve new code for incorporation into the system by devising and carrying out reasonable tests.

This is particularly important after the system has been released for production or maintenance purposes. It is also necessary to keep adequate records showing errors found, changes made, testing carried out, etc. Without such records and the corresponding back-up system, it is very difficult to re-establish working positions if catastrophic failures are discovered.

This type of change control can, of course, be enforced by physical handover of code between originators and the baseline authority, but this is extremely cumber-

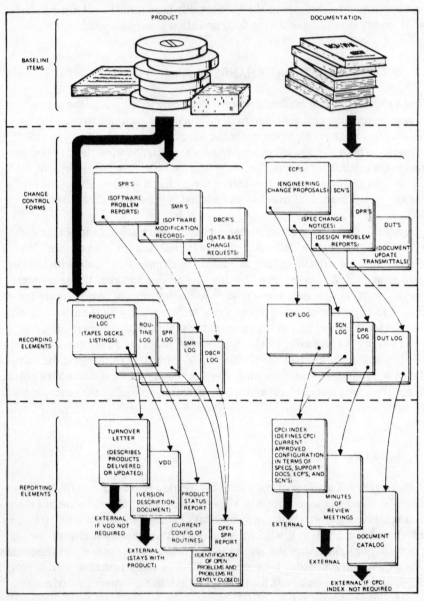

Figure 6.1   A change control and accounting system for a complex development

some and involves manual or semi-manual recording methods as well as implying large teams. The use of suitable development tools as defined in chapter 11 allows different versions of components and systems to exist without sacrificing any control, and can automatically provide the necessary documentation and recording features. This re-emphasises the importance of tools and development systems in the efficient operation of configuration management.

A feature that is of particular importance when many versions of components or systems exist simultaneously is that lists of errors, corrections and support information should be available to the potential users. While these can be kept manually, or as simple computer files for display or printing, the use of an automated CM system can allow such items to be stored directly with the appropriate code and collected and output as necessary.

6.4   CHANGE CONTROL FORMS AND SYSTEMS

For most software developments the controls described above can be implemented without the need for standard forms or bureaucracy, particularly if a CM archive system is used. However, for larger projects, especially those involving other contractors, more formality may be needed.

TRW, which deals with very complex systems, large teams and multiple contractors, imposes a very formal system on developments. Figure 6.1 illustrates the various change control forms employed, the computer-based logs in which actual code baselines and changes are recorded and the various reports that can be automatically produced from such logs. Figure 6.2 shows an example of one of the change control forms.

It must be emphasised that a system of this complexity is not recommended for smaller projects; it would not be cost effective. However, it does show the sort of system that can be constructed where the complexity warrants it and can provide ideas for project managers engaged in multiple contractor projects. Of particular importance is the idea of software problem reports. These provide a method of recording problems encountered that require investigation and may give rise to changes. This idea will be discussed again under the heading of support.

6.5   APPLICATION TO SMALLER PROJECTS

The important point here is to balance the information needed to control versions and to pursue connected changes against the overheads imposed on a small number of staff. The easiest system seems to be a simple standard form on which change requests of all types can be raised and on which progress in approving and implementing the change can be recorded. If this 'form' can be computer-stored rather than committed to paper, so much the better. Such a system can be established during the integration phase of a development and continue unchanged into the maintenance period.

SOFTWARE CHANGE REQUEST

TO Project Configuration Management Office	CONTROL NUMBER . . . .
FROM Name . . . . .Phone	DATE LOGGED . . . .
Firm . . . . .Date	ORIGINATOR'S NUMBER . . . .

CHANGED REQUESTED TO

PROGRAM NAME . . . . .IDENT . . . . . . .PO CONTACT . . . .

Date of Model Change
Required . . . . .PROGRAM OFFICE INVOLVED . . . .

TAPE DISK Ident . . . .

ROUTINE Involved . . . .

REFERENCES . . . .

BRIEF DESCRIPTION (ATTACH ADDITIONAL COMMENTS)	

JUSTIFICATION FOR CHANGE *(Use additional pages if necessary)*

CONSEQUENCES IF NOT IMPLEMENTED

ALTERNATE MEANS OF IMPLEMENTING

WHAT OTHER COMPUTER PROGRAMS ARE INVOLVED?

ARE INTERFACE OR EQUIPMENT PROBLEMS INVOLVED? ☐YES ☐NO (IF YES, SPECIFY)	ARE OTHER CHANGES NECESSARY? ☐YES ☐NO (IF YES, SPECIFY)

DOCUMENTATION AFFECTED

ESTIMATED SIZE OF TOTAL CHANGE = ...(MANWEEKS)		Small	Medium	Large
Small = Less than (1) manweek	Coding	☐	☐	☐
Medium = (1) to (4) manweeks	Testing	☐	☐	☐
Large = Greater than (4) manweeks	*Documentation	☐	☐	☐

FLIGHT LIMITING
☐YES
☐NO _____
(Authorised Signature)

AUTHORIZATION

AUTHORIZED SIGNATURE . . . . .DATE . . . .

FINAL DISPOSITION	FOR CUSTOMER
SCR Processed By . . . . Date	SCR Processed By . . . . Date . . . .

Figure 6.2   Example of a software change request form

7 *Reviews and Inspections*

It was explained in chapter 3 that the achievement of a baseline means the acceptance of the items produced by the previous phase and not just their appearance. In the later stages, when the output is a coded module or an integrated subsystem or system, the form of acceptance is usually the successful completion of a set of previously agreed tests — a subject dealt with in chapter 8. Such testing cannot, however, be applied to such items as specifications or logical designs, but clearly an equivalent mechanism is needed. A design must be validated in some way against the requirements before coding actually begins, for the cost of changing an integrated system to meet forgotten requirements can be orders of magnitude more than just changing the design.

At a lower level, 'front-end loading' is also cost-effective; front-end loading means investment of time and resources in the early stages of a project or maintenance operation in order to reduce costs. Formal specification and design validation is one example of this process. Another is the attempt to ensure that module designs are compatible with outline design before coding begins. A third is assessment of the quality of code before unit testing starts. This chapter is concerned with methodologies and techniques for such operations.

7.1 REVIEWS

Reviews are the milestones of a project, the terms in which planning is done and progress reckoned. A full-scale review will normally consist of the following three steps

- circulation of a completed document for which approval is sought to the reviewing authorities (generally senior technical staff and management, and possibly user representatives); the authorities should have time to familiarise themselves with the context of the documents before any further steps are taken;
- a meeting at which the contents of the document are presented to the reviewers through slides, lectures and question answering;
- a cycle of discrepancy reports and amendments or change proposals to the baseline document.

The actual format of the review will depend on the size of the project and the

phase of the development or customisation. For example, the SADT reader/author
cycle [3] is a semi-formal review mechanism which can be used at low levels or in
small projects to obtain approval for documents. While it is natural to use the
system if SADT is being employed in the analysis or design phase, the basic concept
— circulating proposals under a standard front sheet, receiving comments written
directly on the proposals and iterating until agreement is reached — can be applied
to any type of document, including even code for desk-checking. Such a mechanism
is very convenient in a development team for communication of the user specifications of the system to the software staff for information and comment, particularly if, as is often the case, such specifications are established in separate pieces
over a period of time. The cycle should be supplemented by a more formal presentation of the total user requirements at some stage, to ensure that those responsible
for design of the software fully understand the implications of the system specification. The same process can be used in reverse for obtaining the opinion of
educated users on software design matters.

For large-scale development projects, more formal specification and design
reviews are required. Reference 1 provides details of the sort of reviews common in
large-scale military systems in the United States. Their position in the development
cycle was shown in figure 3.3. An adaptation to less formal development projects
can involve the establishment of review boards at fixed points in the development
cycle that perform in general three separable functions

- review of the overall project and conformance to requirements and financial
  limitations;
- review of detailed technical work done in any particular phase;
- review of plans for future phases.

Depending on which phase the development is in, the balance will differ: to
begin with there will be very little of the second function and a lot of the third;
towards the end the second will dominate. Particularly in the latter case it may well
be worthwhile to have separate meetings of a review board — a general one to cover
the first and last functions plus a separate technical meeting. Such review boards
operate best if supplied with detailed checklists, which need to be built up over
time within an individual organisation. What follows is a list of questions that need
to be answered in order to ensure the successful operation of configuration management. These would need to be expanded to form a full checklist by any organisation
establishing reviews. Individual questions may only be relevant at particular stages
in the development process.

Specifications

- Are the user requirements defined as far as possible, and do they include not
  only immediate requirements but possible future changes and additions?
- Is there an operational configuration management procedure for specification
  control, naming, change approval authorities, etc.?
- Are all relevant documents under change control?

Design

- Is the software sufficiently modular?
- Is the software well structured?
- Is the software understandable?
- Is it debuggable? Do debugging tools exist or are they planned and resourced?
- Have all problems of maintenance or production been solved?

Software Implementation

- Is there an integration plan?
- Is the software design under change control before the start of coding?
- Is there an overall testing and validation plan?
- Are the necessary hardware, software and data for testing modules, subsystems and systems up to and including an acceptance test specified, designed and implemented?
- Are distinct 'builds' of the system defined (see chapter 12)?
- Is a reporting system for technical matters defined and operational?
- Are all relevant documents under change control?
- Does a configuration management system for code modules exist; that is, are versions of modules individually identified; is the use of new versions controlled; are documentation and versions tied together; are test records kept for versions of modules and subsystems, etc.?

Test Control

- Is there an overall test strategy?
- Are there detailed test plans?
- Are the plans sufficient to guarantee the required service levels; that is, are all modules tested with normal, extreme and erroneous input values; are all inter-module interfaces checked; and is each execution path executed at least once (test systems can help here)?
- Are there arrangements for auditing testing and independently evaluating quality?

Installation and Service

- Is there a planned or actual system for dealing with software error reports; has it been checked out during validation?
- Is the handover process from development to maintenance well defined?
- Are there acceptance tests?
- Is there a maintenance plan, that is, provision for development support after production begins?

Documentation

- Is there sufficient and appropriate documentation for
  users
  maintenance
  enhancement
  new version generation
  acceptance test operation?
- Are all ancillary systems documented, as well as the product, for example
  implementation tools
  testing tools
  generation tools
  configuration management tools?

Training

- Have sufficient users and maintenance group personnel been trained in the operation of the system and methods of modification?

Follow-up

- Do methods exist for following up all the recommendations of the review board?
- Do lower level mechanisms exist for reviewing design and code within the project?
- Are an adequate number of lower level reviews scheduled?

The last three questions are particularly important. Review boards can involve large numbers of senior people and take a considerable time. They are therefore infrequent. For them to be effective it is essential that methods of enforcing review board decisions exist and that similar, cheaper, reviews and audits occur between design reviews or other major project reviews to keep individual components on track. All the methods for doing this rely on the proverb that 'two heads are better than one'. The reader/author cycle has already been mentioned; other possible techniques are

- *code reading*: programmers on the same project check each other's code or designs;
- *walk-throughs*: semi-formal review of a design element (or code) by a group, normally of the originator's peers (see reference 18);
- *audits*: independent staff analyse a design or a unit of code;
- *inspections*: a formal technique pioneered in IBM and described in more detail below.

These techniques can be used with less cost between higher level review board meetings. However, it is essential that the higher level review boards satisfy themselves that the lower level reviews are planned and carried out in such a way that problems can be tracked and dealt with at all levels within the project.

7.2 INSPECTIONS

A lower level technique for front-end loading and correcting errors while correction is still cheap is that of inspection. The methodology was evolved by M. E. Fagan. [9] It deals with internal specifications (down to the module level), logical module design and coding, plus the associated documentation and testing. While primarily designed for development projects, the technique can be used equally effectively at checkpoints in a software modification or enhancement during maintenance.

Essentially a series of well-defined checkpoints are isolated in the process of moving from functional specifications to system tests. Examples of such checkpoints are

- design complete; that is, a unit of design corresponds to some defined range of executable code instructions (say five to 20);
- clean compilation of a code module;
- availability of a test plan.

At each checkpoint an inspection of the design, code or plan is made in a formal way described below. Errors discovered by the inspection process are reworked and reinspected before the stage following the checkpoint can be started.

The process is illustrated graphically in figure 7.1. This is a pseudo-SADT diagram showing the activities that take place in the development process between the production of specifications to a functional level, and the presentation of unit-tested modules for integration and functional testing with a defined set of test cases. The inspections carried out to signify the end of each activity are shown as triangular filters on the SADT boxes. Note that each has an inspection, apart from 'unit test', where the passing of the tests itself represents the filter (although a further inspection could be used to check that the test plan had been correctly followed).

Essentially the process is as follows. From functional specifications, individual module descriptions are developed (box 1) and logical designs are then produced for these modules together with unit test definitions (2). From these designs the modules are coded and compiled until a clean compilation is achieved (3) and then unit tested using the predefined tests (4). In parallel with these operations the functional specifications are used to produce a test plan (5) and this in turn is used to generate test cases for use in function and component testing (6).

It is important to note that, at the end of this sequence of events, apart from packaging and publication requirements the product is essentially 'complete'. All the original requirements for the product must have been provided. What follows is merely an extended period of testing, validation and error correction, which may nevertheless amount to half the development cost. The purpose of the inspections I_0, I_1 and I_2 is to measure and influence quality (that is, error content) in the early stages when corrections can be applied more cheaply. Similarly, the test plan inspection IT_1 is intended to find holes or discrepancies in the test plan, while IT_2, the test case inspection is used to discover errors in the test cases (which may otherwise show up as errors in the product during functional testing). Between

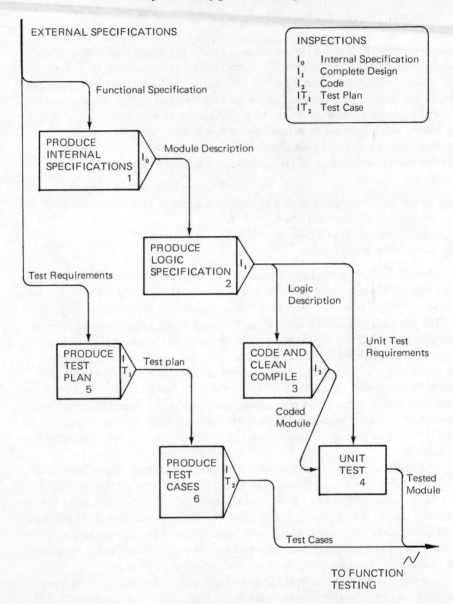

EXTERNAL SPECIFICATIONS

INSPECTIONS

I_0 Internal Specification
I_1 Complete Design
I_2 Code
IT_1 Test Plan
IT_2 Test Case

Functional Specification

PRODUCE
INTERNAL
SPECIFICATIONS
1   I_0

Module Description

PRODUCE
LOGIC
SPECIFICATION I_1
2

Test Requirements

Logic
Description

PRODUCE
TEST
PLAN IT_1 Test plan
5

CODE AND
CLEAN
COMPILE I_2
3

Unit Test
Requirements

Coded
Module

PRODUCE
TEST
CASES IT_2
6

UNIT
TEST
4

Tested
Module

Test Cases

TO FUNCTION
TESTING

Figure 7.1   Inspections in the programming process

them, IT_1 and IT_2 increase the value of the testing that follows both in terms of coverage and cost and can therefore help to improve the quality of the completed product.

For simplicity, the parallel path for program documentation has not been shown on the diagram but similar publications inspections (PI_0, PI_1 and PI_2) can be carried out on documentation.

Unless no errors are discovered, the inspection itself does not constitute the completion of any of the activities. In general, inspections discover errors that require reworking, and it is only when this is completed that the next phase begins.

The effect of inspections of this type will vary greatly with the type of product, the people involved, team and management structure and so on. It is therefore difficult to predict actual advantages. Nevertheless, figures from an IBM experiment for a large operating system component coded in PL/S produced the striking figures shown in table 7.1. Comparisons are made with a similar development that did not use inspections. The increase in productivity in the coding operation takes into account the time spent in performing the inspections and the rework time. Productivity in later phases was also increased due to the higher quality of code arising from the inspection process, but this increase is not included; nor is the resulting reduction in machine time costs in later phases measured.

Application program results are even more striking since, with the use of higher level languages, the time taken for the inspection itself is considerably less. A Cobol program of over 4000 lines compared with a similar, uninspected development (table 7.2) showed a reduction in overall development resources of 25 per cent. More interesting is the pattern of error discovery: 82 per cent *before* unit test, 18 per cent between unit test and acceptance test and none during acceptance test or the first six months of operation.

Table 7.1   Results of inspections in system programs

Increase in productivity of coding operation	23%
Reduction in discovered errors in seven months following unit test	38%

Table 7.2   Results of inspections in application programs

Saving in programmer resources	25%
Errors found before unit test per 1000 statements	38 = 82%
Errors found before acceptance test per 1000 statements	8 = 18%
Errors found in acceptance test and first six months' use	0 = 0%

7.3   FORM OF INSPECTIONS

What follows is the description of the I_1 inspection process. The other inspections follow the same general pattern but differ in such things as materials inspected and number of participants. An outline procedure for I_1 inspections is given in appendix B4.

I_1 inspections normally involve four people with individual roles. They are

- *The moderator*: the leader of the inspection team and therefore crucial to success; he must be able to guide and push the other members when necessary and is responsible for scheduling meetings, reporting results quickly (within one day) and following up on rework;
- *The designer*: the person responsible for producing the design of the program being inspected;
- *The coder*: the person responsible for translating the design into code;
- *The tester*: the person responsible for producing test cases or otherwise testing the program.

The moderator must be a competent programmer, but need not be an expert in the program being inspected. His leadership ability is his most important attribute, and it is often better to choose the moderator from another project or an unrelated part of the same project.

If the same person designs, codes and/or tests the item being inspected, he should take the role of designer, and programmers from related parts of the project take the other roles. The inspection team should normally be limited to four people but programmers of code with which the subject code interfaces may be usefully involved in all or part of the inspection process.

IBM figures for systems programs show that an I_1 or I_2 inspection, including preparation and follow-up, takes about 100 man-hours per 1000 lines of code. While this is not a trivial investment it is still provably worthwhile. Application program inspections take much less time. Experience shows that the effort is best scheduled as a series of two-hour sessions either once or twice a day. It is important that the necessary levels of priority and resources are given to the follow-up to inspections to ensure that problems discovered are successfully dealt with while costs of rework are still low.

An I_1 inspection normally consists of five phases as follows.

(1) *Overview*: the designer describes the overall area of the design and then the specific design being inspected in detail. Design documentation is distributed at the end of the overview. Any rework done as a result of I_0 discoveries, or changes made since I_0 for other reasons are given special attention.

(2) *Individual preparation*: team members individually try to understand the design, its intent and its logic. Checklists of common error types to look for are very useful here. Examples of checklists developed by IBM can be found in reference 9. These will need to be amended and extended in other contexts. Similar lists for I_2 code inspections are also shown.

(3) *Inspection*: the team together inspect the design. A 'reader', normally the

coder, paraphrases the design as he understands it. Every piece of logic and every branch are covered at least once. All documentation must be available throughout the inspection. Any errors discovered are noted by the moderator and solutions are not pursued at the inspection meeting, nor are alternatives discussed. If a solution is obvious it is noted, as is an indication of the severity of the error. The moderator produces a standard written report within one day of the meeting, which goes to participants as well as to the people responsible for updating the checklists for future inspections.

(4) *Rework*: all errors or problems found are solved by the designer.

(5) *Follow-up*: it is up to the moderator to ensure that all required rework takes place. If more than 5 per cent of the design has been reworked, a full new inspection should be held when it is complete. For smaller reworking, the moderator may reconvene the team to inspect the rework or may check it himself.

As a final note, experience shows that modified code in general contains a very much higher percentage of errors than new code. It is therefore especially valuable that modified modules in either a development project or during maintenance be closely inspected. To avoid overheads, several related modifications may be inspected at the same time. Otherwise the processes are identical.

7.4 APPLICATION TO SMALLER PROJECTS

The smaller the team involved, the less important large scale, high level reviews become. Conversely, lower level review techniques grow in importance. The introduction of Fagan reviews into small teams during development or maintenance can produce appreciable improvements in both costs and performance for a very small investment. Indeed this is the only control technique which the author has seen introduced into a wide variety of environments with unfailingly positive results. Apart from the measurable increase in quality they induce, and the overall improvement in productivity, the amount of knowledge and ideas-sharing between team members that is caused by the inspection process often leads to more elegant and maintainable solutions.

The most important consideration in introducing the technique is the attitude of the team. Inspections must be presented and operated as a way of team members helping each other and not as a forum for mutual recrimination. Management must take positive action to prevent any review method from degenerating into a witch-hunt, especially in small closely knit teams. They must also ensure that sufficient time and resources are made available to allow the reviews to operate successfully.

8 *Testing and Validation*

Testing and validation are more closely associated with quality assurance and control than configuration management. Nevertheless, the two control systems are connected, as described in chapter 1. CM is responsible for ensuring that the measuring points required by quality assurance (QA) exist, and this subject has already been covered in chapter 3. In the programming world there is also the peculiarity that software is often used to test other software and the test programs, test data, etc., often need to be specifically produced. This means that the construction of the testing material must be an implicit part of the CM process, as well as the testing itself. This chapter considers these aspects.

8.1 DEVELOPMENT TESTING

It is common practice in software development to leave test definition and production until just before they are needed. This can lead to very bad results, since it means that the tests will often be designed to detect today's (or yesterday's) problems, rather than be concerned with the all-round quality of the item under test. This in turn can mean that modules that have successfully completed all unit testing may fail as soon as they are integrated with other modules, because of lack of attention to interfaces; or that validated, developed systems may fail as soon as users have access, because of lack of attention to possible customer usage.

Such problems can be tackled by specifying tests well in advance of their actual use and, at that early stage, taking into account the wider problems of system quality. Quality assurance staff, if they exist, can approve such definitions, and the subsequent design and implementation. The actual production of the tests can be left to development staff, who will, in general, be more qualified. The actual running of the tests may then be carried out by the development staff, with or without monitoring by QA, or by separate quality control staff, as appropriate to the size of the project, the phase of the development and the importance of the particular test.

The early requirement for test definitions has been briefly touched upon in chapter 2, and the production of various test material is illustrated in both figure 2.2 and table 3.1. Essentially, consideration of testing matters should first arise during the specification of the software. The resulting specification documentation should contain test and validation requirements for the system. With these requirements as a constraint, during the preliminary design period a software integration and test plan should be drawn up covering the period from the end of unit testing to handover of the developed system. This should be in such detail that it allows the individual tests that are to be run during this period to be specified. Implementation of these tests can then take place in parallel with module production. The test plan will also, by stating the level of unit testing assumed before integration, provide the constraints necessary to enable unit tests to be designed.

By the end of the design phase, a complete validation plan down to the level of named tests should exist and should form the basis of all subsequent quality assurance. All test specifications and plans, and the actual test programs themselves, should be placed under change control at the appropriate point. Incorporation of new tests and changes or deletions to old ones should only be allowed with the approval of the authorities relevant to the items being tested. Thus a unit test should be fairly easy to alter but must require the approval of someone other than the unit programmer. A final validation test, on the other hand, should require quite high level approval before it is altered in any major way.

Again, tools can greatly help this form of working. If a composite CM system of the type described in chapter 11 is used, individual tests and expected results can be stored and associated with code units, subsystems or systems and can be controlled in parallel with the system code itself. Such an organisation can also lead to the automation of test running and result comparison.

8.2 HANDOVER VALIDATION

Depending on the project size and organisation, there are up to three parties having an equal interest in the form and success of the final validation, which constitutes the end of the development phase and the beginning of maintenance. They are the development team and management, the quality staff (or possibly user representatives) and the maintenance group to whom the handover is made. All need to be approval authorities for the actual tests used during the validation, and the assessment of whether the product has successfully achieved the product baseline. However, the maintenance group need to have possibly the greatest say in what constitutes the final validation, since achievement of the baseline places all the responsibility for the product with them. They must therefore ensure that all aspects of the product are tested and not just the successful operation of the software system and any associated hardware.

Items which should be given consideration in this final baseline are

● the software product: the facilities and performance of the software being handed over must be fully tested. Reliability should also be assessed, possibly by reviewing validation history, bug records, etc., during the final stages of development;
● support tools: if any special tools have been developed to aid system generation, enhancement, testing or maintenance, these also need testing;

- user documentation: the documentation intended for the user needs both to have its own quality assessed and be checked for consistency against the product;
- maintenance documentation: product design and implementation documentation must be suitable for maintenance purposes, and there must be suitable maintenance and user documentation for any support tools.

In addition, if more than one system version will exist there is also the need to test

- generation ability: the ability to take the software product and generate at least one specific user system should be checked.

8.3   TEST LIBRARIES

Preceding sections have already mentioned how automated or semi-automated testing systems can greatly increase the effectiveness of testing at a reduced cost. One of the prime requirements of any such system is a *test library*, that is, a collection of tests prepared for specific purposes that can be selected according to the attributes of the system to be tested.

Such tests may consist of programs, data, operating instructions or any combination of these things. It is most important that all tests be adequately documented. Not only must the item stored in the library be fully described, together with the aspects of the system it will test, but the necessary environment, run parameters and expected results are also needed. The description of a test will vary greatly according to the product being tested but the first sections of the document shown in table 8.1 can provide a project manager with a starting point for developing his own test descriptions.

Table 8.1 shows the documentation required to describe a *test case*, that is, a particular run of a test. Using a test library, the first sections can merely be references to the library entry supplemented by any extra run parameters. The last two sections of the format specify the actual code being used to run the test and the actual results obtained. This information is completed by the person running the test and can be used for isolating errors, for reconstructing the test after corrections have been made and for historical evidence.

8.4   APPLICATION TO SMALLER PROJECTS

Testing and validation are of equal importance to all projects, regardless of size. The differences of scale apply mainly to the complexity of testing appropriate and the availability of different types of staff. In large projects there will almost always be, beside the developers or maintainers, specific quality assurance and/or quality control staff.

Essentially, QA staff are concerned with the methods and practices used by the

Table 8.1   Possible form of a test case description

Test case description identification: A unique test case description number and title.

Functional capabilities and/or applicable requirements: A reference to and the description of the function(s) being tested. (Requirements transcribed from product specification and augmented or clarified by programmer.)

Purpose: Intent of the test and a sufficiently detailed description of the logic to be tested to fully clarify the purpose of the test.

Test conditions: Identification of any test prerequisites, test materials, special test support hardware or software required, special test setup conditions such as initialisation, and identification of data recording requirements.

Test operations: Detailed sequence of instructions for executing the test.

Test inputs: Identification of test inputs (constants and variables) including discs, tapes or other inputs needed for successful test execution.

Expected test results: Identification of expected computational or functional output.

Test driver: The actual code used to run the test, with the input values as specified in the test case identified.

Actual test results: Description of actual output versus expected output. Description of discrepancies in actual test results to be included.

---

development staff and may establish or approve tests. Quality control (QC) staff will actually carry out their own tests on a product. Small projects will not normally have such staff available, but allowing the developers themselves to specify and carry out all testing is often unsatisfactory. Even if they are scrupulously honest, their detailed attachment to the modules on which they are working will give them a very narrow view of the product and the testing that it needs. On the other hand their detailed knowledge of the system should allow them to construct more thorough tests than any independent QC staff.

A possible way to exploit the advantage while providing an independent assessment at low cost is to appoint a single quality 'expert' within the project. He will be responsible for devising standards to which the system and its components must be tested. Individual developers will then specify tests that conform to these standards and these must be approved by the quality expert. The developers themselves produce and run the tests and the expert approves the results.

This sort of arrangement allows at least one person to be forced to take a wider view of the system and its testing and validation needs, while leaving the actual testing in the hands of those most qualified to do it. With very small projects the quality expert need only be a part-time position.

9 *Internal Documentation*

The technical documentation of a software product is of as great importance as the actual code, since its quality determines the ease with which a developed product may be used, maintained and supported. It is estimated that documentation of a reasonable quality requires 15 per cent of the resources of a development project, and this does not include the work of professional technical authors to produce glossy manuals or advertising material.

Much of the internal documentation generated during a development project forms an integral part of the baselines specified in chapter 3. An indication of the sort of documentation covered was given in table 3.1 in relation to the baselines, and is collected together in table 9.1. Each such document should conform to the change control standards specified in chapter 5. If a baseline configuration management system is in operation, with the required reviews and inspections, the appearance of most of this documentation and its quality will be automatically monitored.

9.1 DOCUMENT STANDARDS

Apart from the change control, identification and status accounting information, it is in general impossible to provide standards for the format and content of each of these classes of document. Indeed, such matters are not really the concern of configuration management. The format of a design, for example, is dependent on the design method used and could be straightforward narrative, design diagrams, data charts or pseudocode. The CM concern is that it should be complete and suitable, and that is taken care of by the reviews described in a previous chapter.

The main concern of this chapter, therefore, is with areas where such external or organisational standards are not imposed, and this reduces to the areas of documentation that affect the individual programmer or software engineer in development or maintenance.

However, it is vital to the success of a software operation that all the documents listed in Table 9.1 are produced to agreed standards and monitored by reviews, audits or inspections. At the start of a project it is therefore essential that there is an agreement reached on the form of, say, the design documentation, and that adherence to this standard is subsequently monitored.

Table 9.1   Internal documentation for software development

Class	Documents
Requirements	Statement of system requirements
Specification	Functional specifications Software specifications Preliminary product specifications Test specifications Module specifications User manuals (draft)
Design	Outline software design Detailed software design Module logic design Test case documentation Production system description
Code	Comments in code Supporting notes, charts, workbooks Link lists, etc.
Testing	Test results Validation results Statistics
Product	Final product specification User manuals Training manuals Production system documentation Maintenance documentation Development and maintenance tools documentation

9.2   PROGRAM DOCUMENTATION

The only sensible way to produce program documentation is in parallel with the program. While in theory it would be possible to take notes at the time that could be tidied up and better presented later, in practice 'later' never happens. There is always another project and other problems.

Nor can the required level of documentation be totally described by the use of in-code comments. Comments are undoubtedly the best way of describing algorithms or the functions of modules, but overall documentation, outline descriptions, transaction examples, reasons for choice of particular methods and so on do not lend themselves to expression in code. And these items are of vital importance to the understanding of the maintenance and production staff who will take over the software. It is therefore necessary for individual programmers to keep other records. A simple way of doing this is exemplified by TRW's programmer's notebook, or unit development folder.[1]

Figure 3.4 shows this item at the top of the documentation list. A notebook is started at the time of the system design review and is augmented and updated until completed at the time of the product baseline.

Essentially, a notebook consists of a loose-leaf binder with section dividers and a standard contents list — see figure 9.1. Other representations are possible — for example, some or all of the content may be kept on a computer file — but the use is the same in all cases. The figure places the notebook in the context of the development activities of figure 2.2. The preliminary design operation leads to an initial version of a product specification, which gives rise to a programmer notebook for each routine or unit. This notebook will be largely empty but will contain sufficient system design information, or references to it, to allow the programmer responsible to understand the requirements and context of his section. In addition, there will be detailed specification documentation of his routine and any supporting information available at that time. As he designs his unit, he will add the sections on detailed design, functional capabilities and unit test descriptions.

The titles and format of these sections will depend on the design methodology used; they could, for example, consist of design diagrams and supporting text, or program design language listings. The actual format and content of a programmer notebook also needs to be customised to the environment in which it is used — the design and implementation tools and the organisation of the development team. Nevertheless, the TRW form can provide a start point. Details of the contents of their unit development folder can be found in reference 1, while figure 9.2 shows a standard cover sheet. Note that the latter provides a link with other control methodologies. The 'due date' column is extracted from the plan and assists with timescale monitoring. Actual completion dates are marked alongside and signed by the originator. The last column for a reviewer's signature and date can be used in conjunction with the inspection system of chapter 7 to ensure conformance with the review procedures. Reference 1 contains several acronyms and organisational assumptions peculiar to TRW's way of working but even the outline presented here should provide sufficient guidance to allow a project manager, or indeed an individual programmer, to define his own system.

The programmer notebook comes into its own during the maintenance period, since it provides a complete record of each unit of the final system and the interlocking of these units is shown by the higher level system design documentation. The notebooks should be kept up to date as each change is made during maintenance so that a complete, up-to-date record is maintained. (There is also a case for applying a documentation system equivalent to the programmer's notebook to a complete development project. This can be used by the project leader to record plans, decisions, reasons, problems, assumptions and estimates, etc., in the form of a log or diary. This is not really CM, however, and it is left as a reader exercise both to decide its form and to assess its usefulness.)

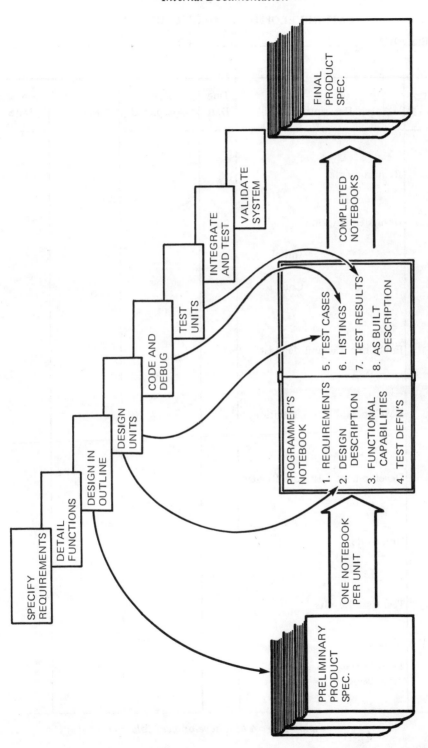

Figure 9.1   Use of a programmer's notebook

UNIT DEVELOPMENT FOLDER COVER SHEET

MNEMONIC _____ CUSTODIAN _____

Section No.	Description	Due Date	Date Completed	Originator	Reviewer Date
1	Requirements				
2	Design Description Initial: Code to:				
3	Functional Capabilities List				
4	Development Test Definitions				
5	Development Test Case Review				
6	Unit Code				
7	Test Case Results				
8	As Built Detail Design Description				

Figure 9.2   A unit development folder cover sheet

9.3 APPLICATION TO SMALLER PROJECTS

The programmer notebook applies to the lowest level of a system, the 'unit', and since even the smallest project has one or more units the idea is as applicable to them as to large units. Since all notebook contents are internal to the project, the problems of a small EDP department discussed in chapter 5 do not apply, and adoption of this method of recording can be recommended to the smallest project. Indeed, an American university teaches the idea to their undergraduate programmers working on one-man projects and not only finds it enthusiastically accepted by the undergraduates themselves, but also that the undergraduates become very saleable commodities to local industry because of their 'discipline'!

At higher levels, even the smallest projects need to record all the information covered by table 9.1, but they are more likely to be combined into a smaller number of documents. The trick here is to decide at the very start of the project: what documents are to be written; when they will appear; who produces them; and how the information of table 9.1 maps on to them. The appearance of these documents and their expected content can be reviewed as part of the appropriate baselines.

10 *Maintenance and Production*

So far in this book we have been mainly concerned with the application of configuration management techniques to software system development. However, after development is complete, CM still has a part to play. Indeed, in its original hardware context, the term 'configuration management' is possibly more usually thought of as applying to this phase. The CM mechanisms are put to work to ensure that the components of a system and their modification state are known at all times, and that any changes made are compatible with each other.

With most software developments, the system that results after the final validation is the only product. The maintenance phase that follows will be concerned only with correcting errors found in this single software system and possibly with changing and improving the system to meet new environmental or user requirements. Any major enhancement may be considered for CM purposes as a re-development and the same baselines and procedures apply. If the original development was done under CM control, the new development will be easier, since existing documents, components and tools may be reused, but essentially the procedures will be the same.

Error correction, involving normally only minor changes to limited areas of the system, is a different matter and requires its own form of controls. These are dealt with below and in chapter 12.

There are, however, software developments that are not followed by a pure maintenance process. The simplest form of such systems are those that are required to be installed on more than one site. Then we have added complications, particularly if the sites' requirements or equipment are not identical. Problems may arise over the applicability of error corrections and the relative priorities of each site. Here strict configuration-management practices are essential to avoid problems. In its extreme form this production process can approach the complexity of hardware production, where the development output is only a prototype or basis system from which widely differing user systems can be generated, produced or customised. Computer hardware suppliers and software product houses are the obvious examples of developers with this type of operation (see, for example, reference 8) but, with the increasing use of distributed processing, even internal DP units my find themselves developing systems to be used on remote machines over which they have no direct control.

This chapter is aimed mainly at the application of CM to such a production environment. The reader who is concerned only with the more usual and more simple maintenance operation can merely skip through it and count himself lucky! The final section considers the simpler case.

10.1   THE PRODUCTION PROCESS

Figures 10.1 and 10.2 are the equivalent of figures 2.1 and 2.2 for a full-scale production process. The following notes explain the operations in the context of CM operations. Figures in parentheses refer to the corresponding box in the diagrams. All of figure 10.1 can be considered as an alternative to the 'operate and support system' activity 33 of figure 2.2.

Produce New Systems (1)

Take 'Order' (11)
In the case of a software sales organisation this could be a real order for a particular version of a system. In other cases it corresponds to representatives of the site on which the system is to be installed stating their needs and wishes. In either case the process must be capable of dealing with change requests and queries arising from later activities.

Specify System (12)
From the initial 'order', possibly after some interaction via the feedback arrow, an unambiguous specification of the required software and corresponding user documentation is produced, together with an equivalent test specification. This is in fact a simplified version of box 1 of figure 2.1. In the worst case, the site hardware may need modification to support the software system. This is also specified at this stage. Again, feedback changes must be dealt with.

Produce Software System (13)
After possible interaction and agreement, a software system must be produced using the latest basis software and any reusable pieces from previous systems. Change requests for the basis or the specification may be produced and errors discovered during validation must be dealt with.

Produce User Documentation (13)
This operation exactly parallels that for the software system.

Validate System (14)
The software and user documentation must be tested, possibly separately at first and then as a total system with the hardware. Any errors found are fed back for processing.

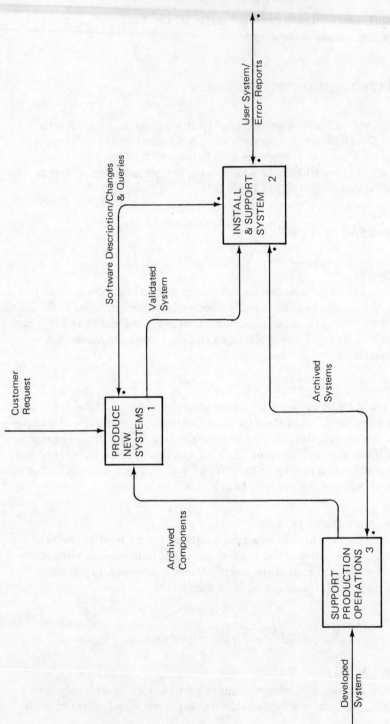

Figure 10.1   Produce customised software systems

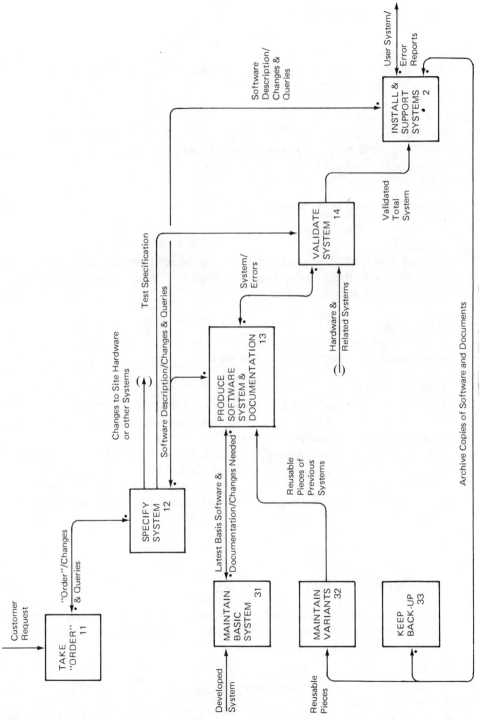

Figure 10.2   Produce customised software systems – details

Install and Support Systems (2)

Install System (2)
The validated system is installed and archived. Any corrected systems are also installed in the same way.

Deal with Errors (2)
Errors found in the installed user system are catalogued and dealt with, some possibly requiring system changes (via boxes 12, 13 and 14) and even basic system changes (via boxes 12, 13, 31).

Support Production Operations (3)

Maintain Basic System (31)
The basic system obtained at the end of the original development is corrected and enhanced, where necessary, under control. Copies of all versions used in delivered systems are kept and distinguished.

Maintain Variants (32)
Reusable pieces of systems and documentation are maintained and distinguished in a form suitable for production of new systems.

Keep Backup (33)
This is a means of reproducing a delivered system when necessary. Systems extracted from the backup archive may be used to evaluate error reports or for despatch to sites by the support activity.

   Note that as for the development model, the diagram is *not* a flowchart and data can flow down arrows and cause activation of a box in a non-sequential manner. The diagrams represent an on-going process beginning with the completion of the basic system development. The configuration management system must take care of all the possibilities of interaction between the activities.

10.2   CM IMPLICATIONS

Considering the software production process in this way, we arrive at the following needs for an effective CM system and associated tools. The need for formal systems will be small at first but will grow rapidly as

- orders increase;
- the base of delivered systems increases;
- the staff change;
- memories weaken.

It is therefore a good idea to introduce these systems as early as possible, even if only a small number of deliveries is expected.

(1) Change control – this falls into two parts

- documentation control: a method of producing, approving, proposing, assessing and approving changes to, and updating all specification documents; the process must be such as to keep all relevant documents in step with each other and the corresponding software;
- software control: a method of controlling the basis software system, user back-up copies and variants so that their content is always known and changes are made only by agreement of appropriate authorities and after relevant testing.

(2) Specification – an unambiguous way of specifying the software and hardware implications of the 'order' and their interrelationships.

(3) Testing – a method of defining testing needs, which is easily transformed into actual validation tests.

(4) Production – a method of producing user systems in the most automatic way, by altering as little as possible and reusing existing components. This requires specialised tools.

(5) Documentation – a method of producing user and internal documentation for each delivered system in the most automatic way, by altering as little as possible and reusing existing components. This requires specialised tools.

(6) Validation – an automated system for storing, generating and running tests and evaluating results for new and delivered systems. A means of dealing with errors found.

(7) Error handling – a system for accepting, cataloguing and processing error reports received after shipping. *This may reinvoke any of the previous operations.*

(8) Delivery – an efficient method of delivering systems, ensuring that all relevant documentation is also sent, and recording actual delivered items.

(9) Archiving – three separate archives are needed, although they may use the same archive system

- basic system: an archive of the latest basic system plus all previous systems still in use somewhere;
- variants: some way of holding reusable pieces of previous systems and extracting and combining them;
- back-up: some way of holding *either* copies of systems delivered to user sites *or* the means of regenerating them.

Note that, in all cases, 'system' means software *and* documentation.

While the basic processes of software customisation and production may be similar in any operation, the actual methods will vary greatly according to the product, for example, according to

- the language it is written in;

- the extent to which individual user systems differ;
- how large it is;
- what the production rate is.

Although all software production processes should contain within them the basic steps of figure 10.2, some steps may be insignificant for some projects. For this reason, although the items controlled by the CM process should be identical, the way in which they are controlled may vary considerably. Again the control methods will be affected by the way in which development of the basis system was carried out. A well-controlled development will automatically generate control procedures and tools that the production manager can take over into production.

While it is therefore possible to produce a checklist for production managers along the lines of appendix B, the result would be much vaguer and less useful. The same effect can be produced by mapping the actual operations of the production group onto the activities of figure 10.2, and then, from the remainder of this chapter, deducing the CM controls needed.

10.3   SOFTWARE PRODUCTION BASELINES

In a similar way to development, looking at the output of each phase of the software production process can help us to determine what the baselines should be. As in the previous sections we consider the most complex case involving individual customisation, as described in figure 10.2. Where production is merely the replication of similar systems, some of the following steps can be omitted.

Each user system produced will have the same baselines. Any production unit will need to have procedures that describe each baseline, how it is to be achieved and agreed and how change control operates. Because there are likely to be several documentary baselines and only one, or at most two, actual software baselines, and because the methods of dealing with each will differ, it is normally best from the procedural point of view to separate documents and software. Essentially one or more procedures are needed for

- definition of the documentary baselines needed, their format and content;
- definition of responsibility for production and change control for each document;
- document change control methods and standards;
- agreement of the 'software completion' baseline, that is, required testing and validation;
- change control methods and authorities for actual software, basis and user versions.

Table 10.1 describes the commonest baselines required in the software production/customisation process. It can be seen that there are essentially four baselines, represented by documents that describe the system in ever-increasing detail from the 'order' to the software design documents. Production of any of

Table 10.1   Software-production baselines

	Baseline	Associated item	Agreement method	Approval authorities	Associated documentation
1	'Order'	'Order document'	Review	Specification agreement meeting	Resource requirements; plans and dates
2	Functional	System specification	Review	Applications, software and maintenance staff. Possibly customer and/or quality assurance staff	
3	Allocated	Special software specifications	Review	As above	Hardware description; software description; validation specifications
4	Design	New software design documents	Audit/inspection	Internal staff	Test plans
5	Unit milestones	Software components	Testing audits	Internal staff	Test results; internal documentation; workbooks
6	Delivery	Software system	Validation	Internal staff, QA	User documentation; delivery registration
7	Handover	Operational system	Customer acceptance	Customer, QA	Archive records

these may require changes to the preceding documents which are handled under control.

Two further baselines are associated with actual code. Unit milestones may consist of a number of internal baselines on individual components, while the whole system is accepted for delivery by passing some form of limited acceptance test, which may often be followed by a further user acceptance test after delivery.

Note that the activity of maintaining the basic system (box 31) may sometimes involve major surgery that amounts to a complete or partial redevelopment. Such operations should be treated as development projects and the appropriate CM procedures applied.

10.4   DOCUMENTARY FORMATS AND STANDARDS

It can be seen from the preceding sections that most of the baselines in the software production process take the form of specifications. Moreover, although simpler, these can effectively be mapped on to equivalent documents in the development process. Precisely the same standards for document front sheets, status information, change control procedures, etc., can be applied to the production documentation as to development documents. Indeed, with only minor changes, the procedures of appendix B.1 and B.2 can be used for either a development project or a production activity.

At a lower level, it has already been pointed out that the programmers' notebooks or unit development folders continue to be of great value after development. A similar system can be adopted for the documentation of individually customised user systems. If the modifications from a standard basis are not large, the amount of re-work needed will not justify one binder per routine, and it may be better to keep a single production folder for each user system. The contents of such a notebook will vary according to the level of customisation required for a particular product and the tools used to carry out the production process. Essentially, though, the same basic sections will be required as for the development notebook, that is

- a statement of requirements of some form and any constraints on the solution;
- a detailed design or modification description;
- source code documentation;
- test documentation;
- updates to system specifications arising from this work (may or may not be part of the notebook).

A particular example of this (recorded in reference 8) was introduced by the author into a group producing highly customised numerical control systems. In this case a *project workbook* is given to the software engineer in charge of customisation, in the form of a binder with a standard front sheet and dividers. The front sheet is shown in figure 10.3. When handed over, the binder contains three sections. Section 1, the version registration documents, are basically an administrative checklist. Section 8, the functional specification, is the statement of requirements for the

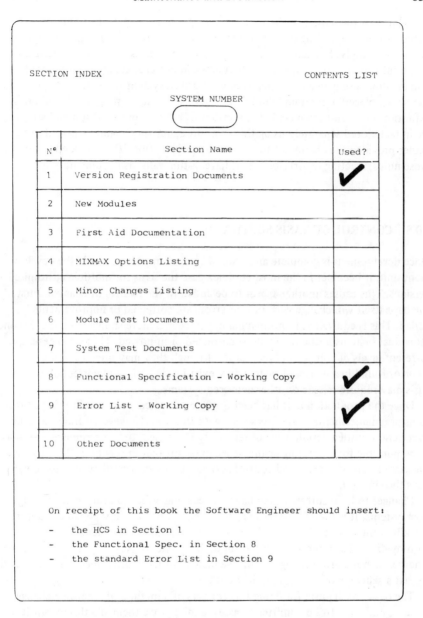

SECTION INDEX   CONTENTS LIST

SYSTEM NUMBER

N.°	Section Name	Used?
1	Version Registration Documents	✔
2	New Modules	
3	First Aid Documentation	
4	MIXMAX Options Listing	
5	Minor Changes Listing	
6	Module Test Documents	
7	System Test Documents	
8	Functional Specification - Working Copy	✔
9	Error List - Working Copy	✔
10	Other Documents	

On receipt of this book the Software Engineer should insert:

- the HCS in Section 1
- the Functional Spec. in Section 8
- the standard Error List in Section 9

Figure 10.3   Project workbook — contents page

programmer. Section 9, the error list, is a standard list of user error categories, which normally needs amendment as a result of the development process. Note that both these are marked 'working copy'; they are used to record, in manuscript, any modifications needed as a result of the production process, which are then used to update the master copies.

Because of the nature of the product, changes may be made in a number of different ways depending on the degree of customisation; the 'design' description varies accordingly. Section 2 (and possibly section 3) is used to record detailed design information for major redevelopments. Minor changes and routine production are done using an automatic, parameter-driven system and details of the parameters are placed in sections 4 and 5. Two levels of test are recognised, and both definition and result are included in sections 6 and 7. Source and system listings are in fact stored separately using this procedure, but they could be placed in the binder provided they were not too bulky. Finally, section 10 is provided to hold those notes, meeting reports, etc., that have lasting value as documentation.

10.5   CONTROL OF BASIS SOFTWARE

Once development is complete and a software system passes outside the development unit, it becomes in the most complex case the basis for multiple customised versions. This causes another aspect to be added to the control of changes. First, the basis itself will change with time as errors are corrected or improvements added. This is equivalent to normal maintenance in a more simple situation. Second, individual systems in the field will be corrected or improved. These changes require different levels of control and recording, although they may interact. For example, an error found in a delivered system may exist in the basis, and correction of the basis may require reissue of other delivered systems.

Once the production unit has been firmly established, responsibility for corrections or enhancements to the basis rests with this unit. However, during the handover period, until a certain level of reliability is reached, the development unit may be responsible for correcting errors. It is important that during both these periods the same levels of control and control systems are used, regardless of who actually does the changes.

Changes to basis software may have far-reaching effects on future or existing user systems. It is therefore necessary to consider carefully any possible changes. Luckily, time is normally available to do this, since urgent problems may be dealt with by direct but temporary alteration to user systems. Not only must it be agreed whether or not a given change should be made, but its priority needs to be assessed so that a schedule of changes can be built up.

The basic mechanism for doing this consists of a method of recording change requests and a control committee to assess and approve them. To this extent it differs little from other forms of change control already encountered, but there is one relatively important new factor: the result of any basis change must take into account the existing delivered systems and must be communicated to those responsible for such systems, to allow them to take decisions on whether to reissue, etc. A form similar to that of figure 6.2 presented to a basis change committee is a standard way of handling such changes. An alternative, simpler form used by the author in a production environment is contained in the procedure of appendix B.5.

The change committee will normally meet at regular intervals during the early life of a product, when basis change requests are frequent. Later they may meet whenever a change is raised.

As with all other change control operations, it is vital that different versions of the basis can be easily distinguished, that known errors, changes and problems in each version are well documented and that associated documentation is updated in parallel. Again, use of automated archives and CM systems can greatly assist in these matters.

When changes are made to a basis system, particularly to correct errors, decisions have to be made on what needs to be done to existing user systems that contain the error. Various possibilities exist, for example

- automatically produce new user systems from the new basis and reissue them;
- automatically reissue at regular intervals based on the latest basis at that time;
- do not reissue automatically but, if a reissue is needed for any other purpose, use the latest basis;
- do not reissue automatically, and only take advantage of the corrected basis if a user actually encounters the error.

Which of these methods, or of various intermediate possibilities, are used, will depend on many factors, including

- the size of the delivered system;
- the similarity of user systems;
- the importance of the error;
- the degree of support required for a new issue;
- the frequency of errors.

It is not possible, therefore, to define a single system to cope with these eventualities, but for any adopted system it is essential that the relationship between delivered software and the existing, supported basis versions be known exactly at all times. Even in the simplest case of pure maintenance of a single system, the problem of introducing system changes may not be simple. A correction to help one user may produce problems for another, and priorities and phasing will be equally important. A change committee and change request procedure will help here.

10.6 CONTROL OF DELIVERED SYSTEMS

Whatever the system used to deal with changes to a basic version, it is absolutely essential that the status of the software that has been delivered to any particular user is known exactly at all times. It is obviously useful to retain an exact duplicate of the customer system within the production unit in some form, but this in itself is not sufficient. When trying to deal with a reported error, or when considering the effect of change proposals on a group of users, it is essential to know how each user system was produced, from what version of the basis software it was generated, what options it contains, what errors have been corrected and so on. The only way to maintain this information is to operate a simple change control procedure on software delivered to user installations.

Essentially the procedure has two parts. When the first version of a particular user software system is delivered to a user site it is *registered*; that is, all necessary details of how it was produced are recorded in a central place. Subsequently, when any changes are made to the customer system, by whatever means, these are added to the record. A register of customer systems may be a manual file or can be computer based. The latter has great advantages in ease of use, and can form one part of an archive maintained by boxes 32 to 33 of figure 10.2.

The basic aim of registration is to record sufficient information to allow the delivered system to be recreated if necessary. Note that this may include knowing the version numbers of compilers and other tools used to generate the system. Indeed, if registration is done correctly there is theoretically no need to maintain archive copies of the delivered system itself, since this can always be regenerated. Actual copies of the delivered systems are only necessary for security purposes. The register will normally be indirect: that is to say, it will not actually contain such items as the customer documentation or the changes made to the basis, but rather will reference them to allow them to be recovered from other archives or libraries. Again, the use of suitable tools during the production process will greatly simplify this. If an automatic or semi-automatic version generation system has been used, the changes made to the basis system can be easily referenced; if the changes have been done manually, a file of all the alterations made will be needed.

Once a delivered system register has been established, it can obviously be used to hold details other than those concerned with system change control — error reports, communications, etc. In fact, it becomes the basis of a user archive.

The delivery of the first version of a customer system is such a major baseline that it is comparatively easy to ensure that the initial registration is made. When subsequent changes are made these can fall into two classes. The first class is that of *fixes*: corrections to urgent problems made by patching the delivered system or similar means. It is vital that all such changes be recorded and this will be much easier to enforce if the register is computer based. The second class is that of *permanent change*, which is made to the source code of the delivered system and normally involves reissue. It is good software engineering practice to insist that a fix is always replaced by an equivalent permanent change in due course.

Since a permanent change requires a formal redelivery, it is normally reasonable to tie the registration process to the other control systems that a delivery requires: acceptance testing, delivery procedures, etc. Figure 10.4 shows an actual example of a multi-part form that can be used as the basis of such a procedure. It moves with the corrected system through the various stages of initiation, software correction, validation and dispatch. At each stage, the person responsible for the activity documents certain details in the associated box and signs-off his section. He keeps a copy of the form so far, and passes the rest of the form to the next person in the chain. The form provides a method of keeping track of a delivery through its various

		DELIVERY CERTIFICATE

System Number: _____   _____

Associated Contract: _____

Delivery Initiated by: _____ Date: _____ Priority: _____

Customer: _____

Customer Address: _____

Attention:

Reason for Delivery:

1. Post-Commissioning System   □   2. New/Extra Copy □

3. Fault Correction   □   Ref.: _____

4. Customer Requested Improvement □   Ref.: _____

Should the Delivery be Charged: Yes □   No □

Software Responsibility: _____ Basis Version: _____

Tape Archive: _____ Ref.: _____ Status: _____

Amendments Archive: _____ Ref.: _____ Status: _____

Functional Spec. Issue Number: _____ Error List Issue Number: _____

Contents of Delivery:

□ Systemtapes _____ off   □ Error List _____off

□ Function Specification _____ off   □ Complete System Document _____off

---

Tape Delivered to QA/Date: _____ Signature: _____

Quality Control: AT □   Read In □   None □

            Date: _____ Signature: _____

   AT Archive: _____ Ref.: _____ Status: _____

Tape Delivered for Distribution: Delivery Group □   Service Group □

            Date: _____ Signature: _____

Delivery Method: _____

Tape Dispatched Date: _____ Signature: _____

Figure 10.4   A delivery certificate

stages and, when complete, constitutes a change-controlled update for the customer system register. Obviously, the individual items in such a form will need modification according to both the software being controlled and the organisation of the production process.

10.7 PRODUCTION QUALITY ASSURANCE

Methods to control quality are as important after initial development is complete as before. The section on inspections has already stated that more errors are found in corrected code than in initial developments. Inspections are therefore a very helpful and cost-effective tool for the maintenance or production manager.

While the equivalent design, code and documentation inspections are equally applicable to major redevelopment or customisation, the timing of inspections may be modified to suit the organisation of post-development work. For example, inspections can usefully be held at the completion of a user system specification, after the completion of the design for a group of software changes needed for a customised system or on the definition of an acceptance test schedule.

Inspections, however, form only one aspect of post-development quality checks. The procedure for defining and producing tests for new releases should be exactly the same as that used during development. It will often not be necessary to retest the entire system in such cases, but care is needed in the definition of tests to check the accuracy of amended sections and to trap any 'regression' of the rest of the system caused by unforeseen interactions. As during development, the tests should be specified early in the cycle. In figure 10.2, the test specification is shown being produced at the same time as the system is defined.

Automated systems are, if anything, even more valuable during this process than during development. For example, the specification could be automatically processed to select or generate test material and scripts. Expected results can be stored with tests and automatically checked against actual results. Test operating systems can be produced to exercise new versions.

Finally, in the most complex production environment defined in figure 10.2, the product groups must also be concerned with validating new versions of the basis. For most purposes, such an operation can be treated as a redevelopment, with checks to ensure that the new basis not only provides the changes required of it but also continues to meet the needs of the production of user systems.

10.8 APPLICATION TO SIMPLE MAINTENANCE

The simplest form of the activities described in this chapter occurs where the manager is responsible for a routine, single-installation maintenance operation. Essentially, his concerns reduce to a single basis system, on which he may be working to produce a new or corrected system, and the actual running software. He is therefore free from the problems of multiple incompatible versions. Nevertheless, a simple form of many of the control procedures and tools may be of help. Particular considerations from this chapter are

- simple change control procedures and forms for the basic software and associated documentation;
- simple documentary baselines for the production of a new software 'issue';

- the continued use of development specification standards for major enhancements, and programmer notebooks for lower level changes;
- an archive system for old versions of code and documentation;
- standard testing methods and inspection procedures for all system changes made, regardless of how (seemingly) trivial they may be.

As in previous chapters the greatest help to introducing the controls necessary without undue bureaucracy or staff demoralisation is by the use of a co-ordinated set of computer-based tools. These are considered in more detail in the next chapter.

11 *CM Tools*

The use of tools to ease both operational difficulties and configuration management, in development and production, has already arisen several times in this book. The following are some examples of the types of tools that can ease the administrative problems of controlling configuration identification and status accounting.

A Development Archive

This type of tool handles automatically the problem of release and version numbering. Each time a new implementation of a particular unit is produced by editing, the differences from the previous version are recorded, and the new version is assigned an appropriate version number. Several such archive or library procedures are available commercially. On top of the archive, automatic procedures can be developed to

- compile a module and test it;
- integrate modules into subsystems and test them.

In such an environment a subsystem may be thought of as the list of module names that drives a system integrator, and this can itself be stored as an archive element. There exist specific tools (such as MAKE [15]) that will not only select the correct items to construct a system but will also ensure, for example, that a recompilation will be performed if a change has been made to the source associated with an object file. Each list can include the version number of each module used, and thus effectively automate one necessary registration process. If, in addition, a tag system is provided within the archive, to allow the reason for any new version of any item to be recorded, we have the basis of status accounting (see, for example, reference 7). The system can also be used, for example, to reference the appropriate issues of the documentation that correspond to the code unit, giving automatic cross-checks.

An Option Generator

Archives can be extended for a production operation to provide a method of holding alternative edits to a particular module, and applying them as necessary to generate versions with particular characteristics and appropriate names. Conditional compilation or macroprocessing can be used to achieve the same effect.

An Interface Archive

This item, based on any simple interactive database system, can be used to inter-relate such items as users, deliveries, system versions, component versions, errors in components and systems and corrections. Such a system handles many of the registration problems and provides a convenient base for statistics gathering.

Documentation Systems

Documentation, whether specifications or user manuals, can be conveniently stored, edited and controlled on a computer. By means of such automation, version number changes and correspondences can be handled with little human intervention, and mismatches can be brought to the notice of those responsible. Many such systems are available, either as stand-alone text-processors, or as systems for general-purpose mainframes or minis. Other, more specialised tools may be useful for producing and vetting lower level documentation, such as code tidiers, code checkers, comment inserters and comment collectors. If the documentation and code can be kept on the same system, as for example with UNIX*, [14] so much the better.

Development CM Systems

Individual tools such as those mentioned above can be combined to produce an integrated CM support system. Such systems can be tailored to an individual project's requirements. Essentially we can store a number of versions of elementary items — source code, object code, documentation, linkage modules, tests, test results, etc. Subsystems and systems also have versions, but their stored form consists of references to lower level items. Figure 11.1 shows a schematic of part of such a system. The code modules A and B exist in various versions whose version numbers show their parentage. (Each node could be just source or just object code with inter-referencing, or could include both.) Documentation for individual modules exists as other hierarchies, and cross-references show, for example, that B version 2.3 is described by version 1 of the corresponding documentation. There are several versions of a system X incorporating A and B and this has its own hierarchical archive structure. A particular entry in this hierarchy consists of references to the components that make up the system. Thus system version 2.1 is constructed of A version 1.2.1 and B version 2.2, and is described by the specification document version 2.

Various access controls can be placed on versions of components or systems to ensure that development versions are not used for production work by mistake.

Production CM Systems

The basis of any production/customisation CM system must be an automatic

* UNIX is a trademark of Bell Laboratories.

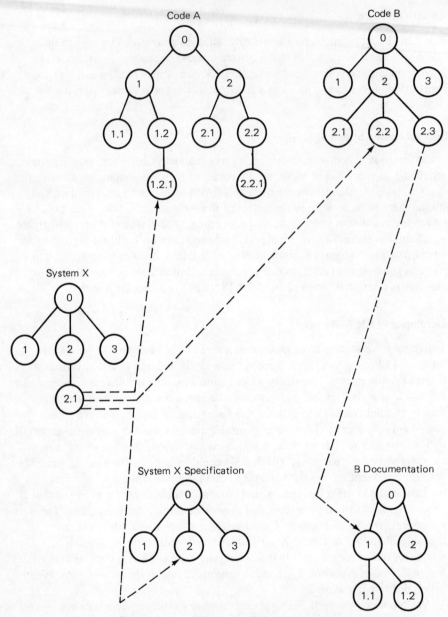

Figure 11.1   Schematic CM support system

archive of the basis software and options, together with tools that will generate particular customer systems from these. Rigorous configuration identification standards are necessary for the various versions of items that exist in the archive, and these can also be supported by software tools.

Possible tools include the following

- a program to list the exact module names, including version and modification level, of all modules in a system being delivered;
- a program to check that source version information and object version information are the same and to print out any discrepancies;
- a program that maintains and prints a log of errors, fixes and other modifications;
- an update program which tracks changes and automatically assigns modification levels.

A software house known to the author developed a system to perform configuration management of this type for a set of compilers. The most appreciated feature of this was that it was based on a time-sharing system by means of which the developers were able to maintain secure files of error reports and modifications that customers could examine at will. This allowed customers to determine the status of problems and fixes without contacting and disturbing anyone in the development team. In addition, since exact source updating statements were maintained in the files, together with appropriate JCL, any customer who wanted a fix earlier than the supplier was prepared to release it could apply the changes to his own system at his own risk. Such a facility may not be of general applicability but shows the type of controls that can be devised.

Obviously, any such system must be dovetailed to the normal development or production tools in use (compilers, editors, etc.). Accordingly, no specific recommendations can be made for specific tools; instead, the remainder of this chapter simply looks at some examples of what is available, to give an idea of the possibilities that exist.

11.1 FORMS AND STANDARDS

CM needs forms to operate. They need not be complex and, in small developments, they can be few. Nevertheless, even in the smallest development, it is a great aid to configuration identification, verification, control and status accounting if information is recorded in a standard way. The aim is not to smother the software engineers in bureaucracy but rather, by providing standard ways of administrative working, to free them to concentrate on real technical problems.

Because organisations vary so much, both in their methods of work and in the degree of standardisation already existing in CM-related areas, the author has always found it better to design customised forms when CM is being introduced. Some examples of these appear throughout this book and its appendices. Some examples of more complex forms in use in other organisations are also shown. Both can be used as a basis for individual design.

An alternative approach, however, is to adopt a fully worked out documentation system that can be obtained commercially, adapting it if necessary to local needs. Normally, such systems cover a wider area than just CM control. For example, SDM/70, a proprietary product from Katch and Associates and Atlantic Software Inc., is a large-system design methodology that includes, as a component part, documentation standards suitable for supporting a CM system. Approaching the problem from another point of view, the British National Computer Centre publish a book [10] which, among standards for all aspects of computer system documentation, includes specification and change control procedures.

Approaching the introduction of CM from such a direction has the advantage that it is seen to be an integral part of the total development/maintenance/production methodology and not as an independent control system that can be imposed on an existing operation without modification.

11.2 ARCHIVES

Basically, an archive is a library-handling program that allows different versions of archived items and, at best, imposes controls on who can access, change or input stored items. Such programs are common in DP installations, perhaps the best known commercially available example being ADR's LIBRARIAN. Many installations implement their own private system, based on whatever file system they use for development. Such a system can provide a sound basis for CM identification and code change control, and provide the foundation on which other CM tools can be built. Ability to store and process text, as well, greatly increases the usefulness of the system.

The choice of an archive system should be much more dependent on the development tools and procedures in use than on CM considerations. The following description of a particular system is therefore not in any sense a recommendation of a form of archive but rather an attempt to indicate how use of an archive system can actively support CM techniques. The system described is a custom-built archive reported in reference 8 and based on Bell Laboratories' Source Code Control System (SCCS). [7]

This archive is a small set of programs that appear to support a huge file into which many different versions of a program or text file can be written, in what appears to be an 'append-only' mode. That is, a new version can be added at the end of the file, but none of the old versions can ever be deleted, changed or overwritten. They are all always available.

The different versions in the file use a hierarchical naming scheme, and a typical usage is as follows. A program, CAT, is written by a development unit and put into the file as version 1. The file looks (conceptually) like figure 11.2a. Development then updates CAT to fix a bug, giving a new version 2 as in figure 11.2b. CAT2 constitutes a releasable version and is handed over to the maintenance and operation group, which puts it into use. Development then continues, enhancing CAT (figure 11.2c). Meanwhile, operations find a bug in CAT2 and fix it, archiving it as CAT2.1, that is, a modification to CAT2 (figure 11.2d). All versions are kept and the relationships are always known. The tree structure can be extended further. Suppose operations fix another bug in CAT2.2, and then generate a version of the resulting system for each of three, differing, remote sites. Meanwhile, development is still enhancing, ready for a new release. We then have a structure as in figure 11.2e.

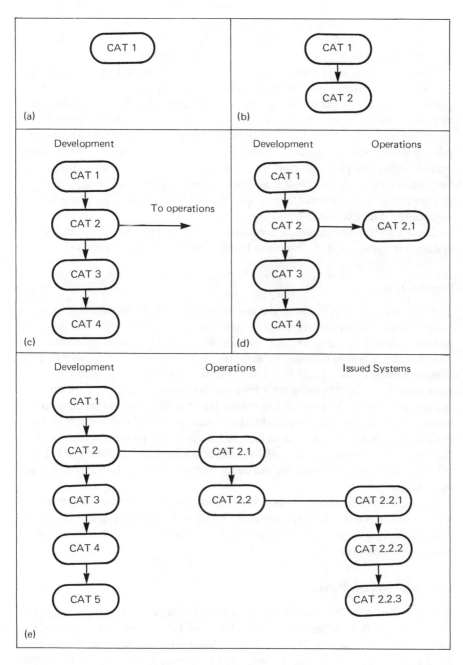

Figure 11.2   A version archive system

Each particular version in the file is tagged with the date and time it was produced, the programmer, the reason it was produced, the bugs it fixed, etc. It is possible to ask the system for a listing of this tag information, use it in other program systems or search it for specific report information.

In practice, such an archive could quickly grow very large and so, following the SCCS approach, when a new version is inserted it is compared with its immediate predecessor, and only the *differences* are actually stored. A particular version can be restored by systematically applying the changes to the base version before output. Since access to the archive is not frequent, the processing time is an acceptable price to pay for the storage saved. It also provides another advantage — the changes made to effect any particular correction can easily be displayed. This provides the basis not only for effective change control but also for assessing how applicable changes made to one version (for example, the bug file of CAT2.2) are to other versions (for example, CAT5).

There are three ways in which development programmers can use the archive system — for program text, changes to baseline builds and specification text.

Program Text

The day-to-day work of the programmers involves the use of the archive to store their program files, to the point that the growing system is perceived as *being* the archive files; that is, adding any improvement to the files should be the central and most important task to be done. To support this, there are automatic procedures to compile a module from the archive and test it, to integrate modules into a subsystem and test it, and to integrate subsystems into a system and test it. A subsystem can therefore be conceived as being a list of module names that drives the subsystem integrator. This list includes the version number of each module and is itself kept in multiple versions in an archive file. Since any previous version of anything can be recovered, any particular version of a subsystem, consisting of (a list of) particular versions of modules, can be reconstructed. Similarly, a system is a list of subsystems.

Putting a build into the baseline is then merely a matter of noting the version number of the system. No other steps need be taken to 'freeze' it, since none of the versions of subsystems and modules involved can ever be changed, but only used to produce new versions.

Changes to Baseline Builds

A large project will often involve release of early builds to other internal groups or to end users; in fact, the last build of a major project may come near the end of the product's life (for example, O.S/360 R21.7). Since it is not always possible to wait for the next build ('release') to fix bugs, even in internal projects, the baseline build must be updatable through change proposals. This is handled quite well by the archive, since any version can be updated, not only the last. If build B is system 5.7, the first change proposal accepted would be implemented as system 5.7.1; the list of subsystems would be the same, except for new version numbers for the changed subsystems. Likewise, if the only subsystem changed is SUBA 9.11.2, the new version would be SUBA 9.11.2.1, with only the version numbers of the changed modules being different.

Specification Text

When conventional, manual methods of document production are used (secretaries and Xerox machines), document files must be maintained. However, if a document-formatting program is used, the documents can be kept in the archive exactly in the same way as program text, with all previous versions available. The archive can optionally indicate which records were changed between a previous version and a current one, allowing the printing of revised documents with 'revision bars' in the margin beside the revisions, calling attention to them. A simple word-processing system consisting of the archive, a formatter and an interactive editor can save a great deal of work in this area.

11.3 DEVELOPMENT AND PRODUCTION SYSTEMS

A development or production system essentially consists of some form of archive with a surrounding set of compatible processors for compiling, editing, etc. Configuration management procedures, as well as such activities as planning control, financial control, etc., can be catered for by either providing corresponding processors or building the relevant facilities into the other processors. The resulting system is sometimes called a software engineering facility and can be represented schematically as in figure 11.3, which is taken from reference 11. The archived material, which includes not only software but documentation, plans, tests, etc., is held in a data base and accessed by the various processors through a software database management system, or SDMS.

Such a conceptual system can be built up pragmatically over a period of time once a sensible archive system has been established. For example, the French company CSL [12] have built upon their version of ADR's LIBRARIAN a series of tools for both technical operations and financial and management control. A more acceptable alternative in some situations is to build a total purpose-designed system. Such a system is described in reference 13. While initially produced for microprocessor software development, it has since been used for other purposes. Called MSEF, it is based on the UNIX [14] operating system on a PDP/11 machine.

The most interesting facet of this system is the power of the database, which is implemented using the UNIX file system. Basically, there is a tree structure that allows systems to be built up of subsystems, etc., down to a module level at which source is held (figure 11.4). There is also a leaf associated with the system called a LOG leaf, which records all changes to the system tree. This simple tree form is extended to allow other leaf and node types to be stored. For example, at the

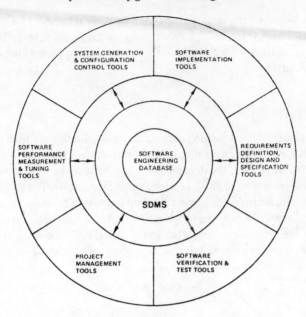

Figure 11.3   A software engineering facility

lowest level a module or routine node may have not only a source code leaf but also

- the corresponding object code leaf generated by a language processor;
- the listing and symbol tables produced by a language processor;
- textual documentation of the routine, which can be processed by UNIX;
- a property leaf giving financial, management and CM information;
- design specifications for the routine;
- a test node referencing a test driver, test data and test results.

Moreover, several different versions of at least the source, object, listings, test items and text can be held. Again, at the intermediate subsystem or system node levels we may store, for example

- linker commands for constructing the subsystem from the routine object codes;
- actual linked modules and listings (again in several versions);
- a property leaf;
- 'include' nodes to incorporate external source;
- multiple textual nodes for specifications, manuals, etc.;
- design specifications.

Other, special-purpose nodes and leaf types can be defined by the users. An example of a total system entry is shown in figure 11.5.

Finally, it is possible to have several system configuration trees in the same MSEF and to allow controlled linkage so that specific nodes or leaves can be

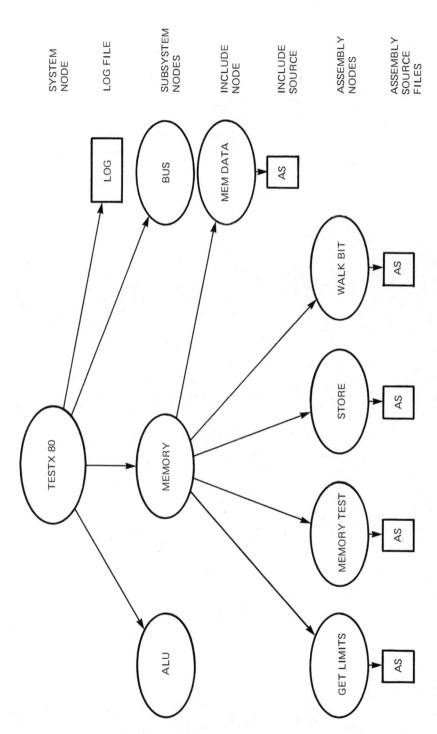

Figure 11.4   MSEF database structure

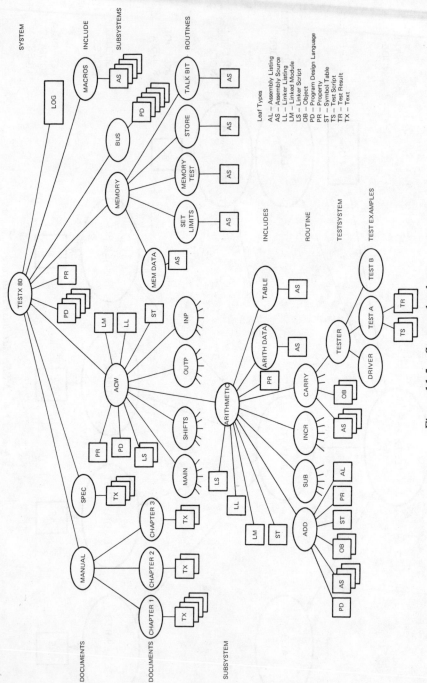

Figure 11.5   System database

shared. This provides the same sort of facilities for parallel operations described in section 11.2 above.

All the processors used in the project to which MSEF is applied work directly on database items and return results to the database where appropriate. Thus, to construct a system, only the relevant node needs to be referenced to provide all the necessary driving information required by the processors.

Such a system is obviously a powerful tool for the software engineers who use it, but its CM advantages are also very powerful. Records are kept automatically; changes to specifications, code or documentation can be monitored by access control; interrelations between items can be automatically maintained; and all this without any extra work on the part of the programmers.

11.4 PRACTICAL APPLICATION

The use of tools is one area where the manager of smaller projects is at no disadvantage with respect to his colleagues with more complex tasks. Even the smallest project team will have some development tools, and judicious additions and modifications can provide very large control benefits. For example, in one installation a simple modification made to a source library system prevented any further access of a particular module after it had been copied out, until a revised version had been returned. This completely solved a serious problem that the installation had previously had with multiple, indistinguishable versions in circulation.

Moreover, in a small team the introduction of new tools becomes much easier and the inertia to change is less evident. Indeed, managers should wherever possible try to introduce tools that induce formal working methods rather than attempt to introduce formal working methods that can then be backed up by tools.

Whether the team is large or small, the most important thing is to establish a coherent strategy for tools that allows them to interact in a sensible way and to support the overall life-cycle and control methods desired by the manager. While individual tools can be helpful, an integrated system of tools and operational methods greatly amplifies the value of each of its components.

It is difficult to provide examples that will be of interest to more than a very small proportion of the readership. Normally, the choice of development or production hardware will in turn determine the availability of tools. Development teams for systems based on IBM mainframes and INTEL micros will have the same CM-associated problems but the forms of solution open to them are very different. The only process available to the would-be introducer of CM techniques is to

- produce his ideal life-cycle model;
- from this, determine the tools he would ideally like;
- match this 'shopping list' against what is actually available on his system;
- modify the life-cycle accordingly.

For the lucky manager who can choose the development system he needs, serious consideration should be given to UNIX [14] or UNIX-like systems. It is no coincidence that several examples in the preceding sections have been UNIX-based. UNIX was designed as a development system on Digital hardware and was from early days used as an environment to develop programs for other hardware and systems (IBM, CDC, Xerox) via the programmer's workbench. It provides very good facilities for building private tools and incorporating them into the existing system. Its undoubted attractions are emphasised by the recent appearance of many UNIX 'look-alikes' for various hardware, and the work done at the Lawrence Berkeley Laboratories to provide a UNIX-like interface for program development on a variety of machines.[16]

12 *Organisation for CM*

This final chapter is concerned with the organisation of both work and people that can aid the introduction and operation of CM in software projects.

First, we address the work that needs to be done by a project leader when a new development is initiated. Second, we consider the organisation of development activities. Then the interfaces between the development and maintenance or production activities are covered, as are the interfaces with users, with accent on error handling. All three are closely connected, since the final "user support systems" must normally be considered at least in outline at the very start of the project. From this we go on to examine staff organisations and finally look at the problems of introducing CM into a software organisation.

12.1 PROJECT INITIATION

An earlier chapter has already introduced the development CM checklist of appendix A, which is a series of questions designed to cause a project manager to think about all the CM-associated items that must eventually be covered by his project. However, some of the answers to those questions will only be completely available towards the end of the project, although the work necessary to determine the answers must be planned quite early on. In this section we are concerned with the initial steps of a project manager at the very beginning of the project. It may be helpful to look again at figure 2.2, the development process, before continuing further. Note that we are *not* concerned here with the actual technical problems of the project, nor directly with planning and resource matters, but with control and management aspects that affect both of these technical and administrative areas. The following are the general questions to which the project manager should obtain answers at a very early date.

Project Definition

What are the external documents that determine what this project has to do? Are they complete? Are they agreed? From whom do I obtain extra information? With whom do I negotiate changes? Are the documents under change control? Is this a one-off development or a basis for future production? What actually has to be 'delivered' at the end of the project?

The answers to the last two questions in particular will greatly influence the way in which the project is carried out. In internal DP departments it is perhaps useful for a project manager to obtain an 'order' for the software from some other unit (a user group or representative) in exactly the same way as commercial organisations receive customer orders. This determines exactly what he has to deliver and also establishes a 'customer' for him to negotiate with. This can sometimes make up for the lack of formality that otherwise normally ensues.

Organisation

What groups of people are to be concerned with the development and what are their responsibilities? Is there some form of steering committee? What level of control are they to have? Who will do design reviews? To what level are they to be involved? What are the relationships with other staff groups? Who are the contacts?

The answers to these questions are essential to the establishment of any CM system. The known and agreed responsibilities of the groups involved will determine the way in which baselines are agreed, and the change control and configuration management responsibilities of each group. One or more Change Control (or CM) Committees will need to be established. These can form a useful management tool.

Baselines

What are to be the baselines of this project? What constitutes each baseline (detailed list of documents, status, builds, etc.)? How is each baseline approved and by whom? How much of figure 3.4 is actually to be applied to this project?

The detailed contents of each baseline must be determined at the very start of a project and should be major steps in the overall plan. Remember that the achievement of a baseline must be the acceptance of all of its component parts, not just their appearance. If a baseline item is to be a draft or preliminary version of something, its minimum content and agreement status must be stated.

CM Procedures

What standards are to be adopted for documentation production and agreement? What change control system is to be used? Who are the relevant change control authorities? How are the product items to be named? What naming conventions, version numbers, etc., are to be used? How is code to be change controlled? How is testing to be done, and by whom? How is validation to be done, and by whom? What internal reviews and inspections are to be used in the project, and at what points? What internal documentation is to be produced and how is it approved/tested/validated?

This set of questions essentially determines the CM procedures that are to be adopted. All must be ready and known by all team members before development work proper starts — it is almost impossible to apply such standards after the event. The level and scope of application in in-house organisations will often be determined by the interest that outside users can be provoked into showing.

When the project manager has answers to all these questions, the CM systems for the project can be easily established. Other, non-CM items may, however, also influence working methods and controls. Examples are the reporting requirements on progress and resource usage, and planning methodologies. With good CM methodology in use, both these areas become easier to handle, since control and visibility are both improved. The technical standards adopted − language, design methodology, etc. − will also impact the actual control, review and inspection methods. Finally, the handover matters described below may also influence project milestones.

12.2 BUILDS

Any implementation larger than about 1,000 lines of code can profit from being done in planned stages called *builds*. A build is a complete and running version of the system in which some of the functions are bypassed or some of the implementation constraints not yet met. For example, an early build of a compiler might handle only a few statements in the language and take more memory space than desired. Missing functions are handled by stubs that simply report that the function has been requested and bypassed. Note, though, that a build should be 'complete' in some sense, for example, a perfect syntax analyser with stubs for all code generation does not constitute a good build, since it would not bring into play all the functions that make up a compiler. A complete compiler able to accept only a very limited language subset would be much better.

Division into builds has advantages both for the implementors and for management. For implementors, it provides an earlier check that the basic structure and algorithms are usable. It also gives them, in the previous build, the solid base of a working system on which to construct the next build. This reduces the problems that arise when several programmers simultaneously update a system. Instead, each can have his own version of the previous build, and change it in isolation.

For management, division into builds provides a much more accurate measure of progress. It is a well-known fact that a system being implemented 'all at once' will quickly reach the level of '95 per cent finished', and then stay there for a long period. Each build, on the other hand, must be 100 per cent complete to be accepted, thus indicating precisely what has been accomplished.

To be useful, each build must be precisely defined and scheduled in a document called the *build plan*, which states in detail what functions each build will support, what implementation constraints it will meet and what tests it will pass, all by reference to the system functional specifications and the system test requirements. It also defines the amount of work estimated to be needed to go from one build to the next. Build operations are usually associated with a top-down integration strategy.

To eliminate any extra work caused by the division into builds, it is necessary that the functions added in one build be as far as possible independent of those in the others, and that the effects of implementation constraints be isolated in one place. In our compiler example, each statement type should be handled by a separate subroutine. Also the fact that the first build is too big cannot be caused by all of the code being too big, but must be caused by something like keeping an intermediate file in memory. The file handler in this build would simply move records in memory, and in a later build would be changed to do I/O, without changing its interface.

The build plan is quite closely connected to the system design specification, and the two are generally done at the same time. On the other hand, changes to the build plan are usually treated somewhat more casually than those to the other documents. However, the builds themselves, once accepted, are maintained under very strict change control. Some builds may be controlled at higher levels than others. For example, the first and last build will normally be subject to high level review and steering committee controls, while other builds will normally be of concern only inside the project. This is, of course, because the first build contains the basic system structure, while the last build is the system itself.

(Note that an extra advantage of a build strategy is that the last-but-one build is often a good fall-back system in the case of slippage, and does not require extra resources to produce.)

12.3   DEVELOPMENT HANDOVER

When a software product is to be handed over to a user, it must normally first pass evaluations or acceptance tests designed to prove that it is fit for the purpose for which the user intends it. Similarly, when a product development is complete it should also be evaluated for its fitness for use as a maintainable, supportable product. This may involve quite different considerations. Some examples are the following.

Maintenance/Production Documentation

At the very least the maintenance team must be able to find their way around the software. In the case of a software system intended to form the basis for production, thought should have been given in the design to the way in which installation-dependent options can be dealt with. For each such option taken into account in the development, there needs to be a description of how it will be specified, an indication of the areas of software affected and details of the actual form of changes needed.

Maintenance/Production Archive

It is of little use to hand over to a maintenance group the absolute binary of a particular system as a basis for future maintenance and enhancement. It is not even enough to hand over the corresponding source. It is part of the responsibility of the development project manager to ensure that the group receive something that is capable of being the basis for their operations, and this will normally mean establishing an archive of some sort for the software that can be used in the post-development environment. All items in the archive should be suitably identified according to the CM system used in development, which can then be carried over into the production phase.

Maintenance System

At the very minimum, the way in which the production group is expected to set about maintaining the user system must be obvious. If standard available tools, such as linkers, compilers and file systems are intended to be used, this is all that is needed. However, particular products may require specialised tools for option production, test generation and running, and new feature development. Other products may use existing tools in specific combinations or in non-standard ways. In such cases the maintenance system needs to be documented and verified to the same levels as the developed system itself.

The maintenance or production phase of a successful system goes on for much longer than development. In terms of savings, therefore, it is essential to make it as efficient as possible. The basis of any successful post-development operation is a set of good, interacting maintenance tools. These must be supported by procedures to deal with the interfaces necessary for end-users of the delivered system. These are outlined below.

The essential procedures must deal with

- error reporting and correction;
- control of changes, versions and customer systems.

12.4   ERROR HANDLING

However good a software development, the delivered system will contain errors. While trying to reduce the errors to a minimum, it is also necessary to prepare for their discovery. Basically, well-defined procedures are needed for the following functions.

Error Reporting

There must be a simple, well-publicised method for a user to report a suspected error. This should include not only the place to which the report is made, but also the information that must accompany the report. Standard forms are usually essential for this purpose. Priority reports by telephone or direct contact cannot normally be avoided, but should always be followed by a written form. An example of such a form is shown in figure 12.1. This also provides space for recording the analysis and correction of a problem. While intended for external customer-discovered errors, a change to the first box makes it equally applicable to internal

	SOFTWARE DISCREPANCY REPORT	Page of
		Date

Customer (name, address)	Originators reference

Program affected (name, ident na, release no, release date)

Computer configuration

Problem description

Problem classification:

☐ Catastrophic failure   ☐ Functional problem

☐ Functional error   ☐ Documentation faulty

Enclosures (discrepancy verification):

☐ Program listing   ☐ Object program   ☐ Dump

☐ Other listing   ☐ Test material   ☐ Other

Comments

RESPONSE

Analysis of problem	Corrective action	Endosures ☐
		Reg. no.

Figure 12.1   A software problem reporting form

developments. The same form and procedures can be used during the validation period at the end of development (a useful check that they are workable).

Error Diagnosis

Once an error report has been received, it must be dealt with quickly to determine its cause. Responsibilities for this operation must be clearly stated.

Priority Assignment

When a genuine software error has been diagnosed, the correction, unless trivial, must be given some priority and a plan produced for its implementation. It must also be decided what form the correction will take — a quick fix, a permanent correction and a reissue, or the first followed by the second. It is normally sensible to have priority assignment done at a regular error meeting that considers all outstanding reports. Such a meeting must also concern itself closely with change control — see, for example, the procedure of appendix B.5.

User Contact

This must be at two levels. For a user who has actually reported a suspected error, it is essential to keep in contact at regular intervals throughout the diagnosis and correction period to show that his problems are being dealt with, even if immediate progress cannot be reported.

On a wider basis, it may also be necessary to broadcast, generally or selectively, to users details of known errors, suspected errors, avoidance action and proposed corrections. This can be done by direct contact, newsletters or accessible computer files as described in chapter 11.

Control Procedures

The exact status of changes and errors must be known at all times, and if corrections are to be made selectively to individual sites it is essential to know which corrections are compatible with each other. Such information is best recorded in a computer-held database that can keep track of the relationships.

Statistics

If the error meeting described above and the associated change control authorities are to do their work adequately it is necessary for them to have up-to-date statistics on errors and associated performance matters. Such information can be collected and presented automatically from the sort of database described under control procedures.

12.5   ERROR CORRECTION

Before any system goes into use, the ways in which corrections can be applied must be known and supported. A whole spectrum of possibilities exist, including the following.

(1) Patches on site: these are normally undocumented, untested and therefore uncontrollable, and very dangerous. They should only be used when unavoidable, and always followed by a more formal, controlled and tested correction.
(2) Corrections on site: provided specific updating software is available, corrections can be sent and applied on site. The form of the updating software can vary. It may, for example, be a program that can read an issued program file (whether binary or source), apply corrections and create a new file. It must also, for control purposes, be capable of altering the version identification, and it may also have the ability to check for consistency, for example, that correction 1 is applied before correction 2. Alternatively, the issued system may itself contain the facility for self-modification by correction parameters after it has been loaded. Such parameters should also change the in-core identification.
(3) Reissues: the alternative is complete or partial reissue of the software system. This provides the most positive control. This is fine for small systems or systems where reissues and possibly reconfiguration have been taken into account in the design, but otherwise it can prove expensive.

Any sort of error correction system must, of course, be closely tied to the registration and configuration control systems, so that at any time it is known exactly which version of a product a user has and what its properties are.

12.6   ORGANISATION OF STAFF

Organisation is subject to a range of pressures completely outside the CM spectrum. However, it is worthwhile to state some basic points that arise from CM considerations.

First, development must be separate from maintenance or production. This is not to say that the same team cannot do both, but that there must be a formal handover process between the two phases as described in section 12.3.

Where possible, groups should be divided according to the type of controls that determine their work. For example, consider the production process of figure 10.2. Maintaining the basic system is subject to long-term forces determined by errors, enhancement and the market place. Producing an individual system is subject to the more immediate pressures of a specific order, while supporting a customer is subject to the instantaneous controls of telephone calls and error reports. Given two controls, the short-term one will almost always win out. It would therefore be foolish, for example, to have one group of people or one person responsible for both maintaining the basic system and dealing with customer queries; the combination of either of these tasks with the production of specific systems would be more sensible, and complete separation of responsibility with interaction between the three groups better still.

(As an aside, it is interesting to note that many of the modern techniques for producing structured systems and programs can be applied to determine a sensible structure for a human organisation. Not only do some system analysis methodologies — see, for example, references 3 and 5 — adapt equally well to the analysis of non-computer systems, but the underlying techniques of many structured program methodologies can be applied to determining a structure for a human organisation. Examples of such techniques are

- structured design: deriving the 'modules' of the organisation from the data flow to reduce functional interactions;
- information hiding: restricting knowledge of particular data or information to the units that control it;
- input/output structure: structuring the organisation to mirror the flow of information and data into and out of the group.)

Whatever the organisation, it is essential that all groups in production and maintenance use the same CM procedures and tools, and even better if these are a superset of those used in development of the product.

The ideal organisation should, of course, be functionally based; that is, there should be separate groups responsible for each separable development or maintenance function. With small teams this is impossible. Nevertheless, it is often sound practice to make an individual *responsible* for some function even if he does not do the work associated with it. As an example, consider validation. All logic says that system validation should be carried out by a different group of people to the developers. In the large organisations where CM originally evolved, these were the quality assurance or QA group. A small team cannot afford such a luxury, but at least some of the benefits can be achieved by allowing the developers to do their own testing and by appointing someone responsible for inspecting and approving their tests and vetting the results. As described in section 8.6, such a person will often take a wider systems view and uncover holes in the testing strategy that the individual programmers overlook. Similarly, appointing somebody responsible for accepting the system for maintenance, even if the original development team are actually going to maintain it, can be very cost-effective.

It is essential that all staff involved in any stage of development or production be adequately trained in the methods, tools and techniques needed for their particular job. For example, on a large project with separate development and maintenance teams

- one (or more) of the developers could continue working on the project in the maintenance phase;
- a training program could be used to prepare maintenance staff;
- members of the maintenance staff could participate in earlier stages, particularly integration;
- best of all, all three methods can be used.

Qualifications of reviewers are particularly important. At any development phase, one of the reviewers must possess at least the same skills as the creators of the item being reviewed. In addition, at each formal review point, it must be possible to review the software critically and constructively in all of the following contexts

- user requirements;
- status versus schedule;
- status versus budget;
- quality assurance;
- CM;
- overall product plans.

Often formal training is required to achieve this.

12.7   INTRODUCTION OF CM

The author has been involved in the introduction of CM procedures, methods and tools in a variety of differing environments and with varied results. The experience suggests that CM is a very valuable weapon in the software manager's armoury but that its introduction must be carefully planned and executed. This section considers the management aspects, while the next and final section considers technical problems which should be avoided.

(1) CM must blend with any other control systems in use in the organisation. Any duplication of effort will cause automatic rejection. This means that actual procedures must be custom-built.
(2) Procedures supported by tools that also provide technical advantages are much easier to introduce than pure procedures that are seen as a management over-head.
(3) CM cannot be imposed unilaterally from above; it has to be at least accepted from below. This means an investment in education and training.
(4) While a complete CM system of interlocking tools, procedures, standards and methods should be designed in outline before introduction, the actual implementation should be sequential over quite a period of time. It is worth-while getting individual items such as reviews or change control fully operational before introducing others.
(5) Someone with sufficient authority must be given responsibility for the introduction of CM. The introduction must be an identified, budgetted and resourced activity.
(6) The best CM salesman is a successful practitioner. In the author's experience the best way to introduce inspections into an organisation, for example, is to find a reasonably sympathetic team or subgroup and overwhelm them with support for the introduction. The results that this generates will cause other teams to come and ask whether they can use inspections, too.

(7) Last in this section, be sure to tailor the CM system to the organisational requirements and available resources. Introduction of new working methods takes time and money, and it is better to go for a limited but achievable objective than to attempt to achieve all the possible advantages of CM and fail. It is much easier to introduce new methods when a bridgehead has been secured.

To take a specific example, let us consider the introduction of CM techniques to a data processing department of around 30 to 40 people organised into project groups of 5 to 10.

The first step will be to establish a model of the 'ideal' life-cycle of a typical project within the department. This should cover all phases from initial requirement through development to maintenance and final disposal. It should show not only technical activities but financial and other management controls. The figures used in earlier chapters can be used as a basis, but each organisation will be slightly different. From this model it will be possible to establish

- the major phases, to establish baseline points;
- the information interchange needed to establish baseline contents;
- the quality assurance process required to establish the position and form of reviews and inspections;
- the usage of current tools and the need for new or changed tools.

Even within such a department, individual projects will vary, but it should be possible to determine an overall model with alternative sections for projects of particular types. All members of the department, even the most junior, should be asked to review this model and comment on omissions or irrelevancies, and to state priorities for the introduction of new tools or methodologies.

From this point it should be possible to draw up an outline long-term (five-year) plan for the introduction of new tools and methods into the overall department, and a more detailed 1-year plan for the introduction of around three items only. These first items should be chosen to give maximum obvious benefit to both management and workers. Basic tools, such as the introduction of a powerful development and production archive, are good candidates, since they have both stick and carrot properties: they provide much better control of work, while at the same time removing tiresome chores. Methods with low introduction cost such as inspections are also good candidates. The tools or methods should provide a springboard for the later stages of the introduction plan and should be chosen with this in mind and not in isolation, but their own immediate benefit should also be very clear.

For each selected item for introduction, a project team should be chosen as the showcase project. The choice may well be very limited. For example, a new development archive or configuration identification system may only be used by a project that has just started up. Programmer notebooks or inspections could be introduced at later stages in a project life. With a team of the size stated, it would be wise to devote one person to assist with the introduction of the tool or method, to review its use and progress continuously with its users, and to modify it accordingly; in short to overwhelm them with support. It is unwise to introduce more than one new way of working to a project at the same time, unless they are closely inter-related (for example, specific tools to work on the archive) or greatly separated (for example, controls applying to different phases of the development cycle).

Once a good development archive is in operation, with the imposed configuration identification methods that it implies, it will be easier to introduce control and status-accounting procedures. These should have a direct correspondence to the position and status of the corresponding item within the archive. The movement from one status to another within the archive can then provide a platform for the introduction of review and quality-assurance procedures.

At the end of the project (or the appropriate project phase) there should be a review of the effectiveness of the tool or method and, on the basis of this, changes should be made. The updated item can then be introduced to other projects using the initial project team both as a 'reference sell' and a support base. At the end of the 1-year plan the 5-year plan should be reviewed and amended accordingly and a new 1-year plan established. With a well-planned and supported first year, each successive year will be easier. The sign of a successful CM introduction is when every staff member considers it to be the normal way of work and what he would have done anyway if left alone.

12.8   CM PROBLEMS AND PITFALLS

Finally, this section looks at the things that can go wrong with CM. Although configuration management offers many advantages to a software project, it must rely on the good judgement of those who plan and implement it. The following are some common hazards to avoid:

Documentation Out of Step with Programs

If the master tape, deck or disk and the related product documentation are not controlled and changed as an integrated package, their compatibility cannot be assured. The configuration on tape, deck or disc can change as a result of error corrections, while the associated changes in the documentation may not be incorporated. Careful monitoring is needed to avoid this.

Misplaced Control

Software can be either over-controlled or under-controlled, and controlled either too soon or too late. Too many or too few reviews and approval signatures may be required for a particular type of change and the level of review and sign-off may be too high or too low. Approval authority for changes should be adjusted according to the time in the development cycle, the nature of the change and the scope of the change. Depending on the particular combination of time, scope and nature, the appropriate approval authority might be the programmer, the project manager, a steering committee, a design review board or all of these. Getting the balance right may be a matter of trial and error, and there should be controlled flexibility in the early days of CM introduction. If you get it wrong, don't be afraid to change it.

Unnecessary Paperwork

Excessive paperwork can result from dividing a software product into too many controlled units. Baselining too early also results in extra paperwork. Many other planning decisions can affect the amount of paperwork required. Paperwork should be kept to a minimum in the early stages – it will always grow.

Undocumented and Circumvented Procedures

Undocumented procedures are not easily learned, followed, monitored, modified or analysed. However, well-documented procedures can still be circumvented. Circumvention of the more critical steps can be minimised through special techniques, such as computer checking for authorisation before allowing updates to configuration-controlled systems.

No Backup

A project should never rely on only one copy of a configuration-controlled master system. Duplicates that are validated by bit-by-bit comparison should be kept, and carefully controlled.

No Low-level Reviews before High-level Reviews

Entering a high level review or audit without adequate preparation can be awkward, and can produce delays. Preparatory in-project review or audit can catch existing or potential problems before the major review does. Occasional temporary use of highly experienced technical and management personnel from outside the project for independent reviews can also be helpful. Project personnel can be too close to the review material. Inspections (chapter 7) can be helpful here.

Deferred Approval of Development Specification

Delay in approving a development or product specification can be costly if the user requires changes that affect current design, and judges these changes to be within the scope of the 'contract'. Every attempt should be made to fix specifications at the earliest possible moment and make changes only under control. If users will not participate even when encouraged, they should at least be made aware of the 'freezing' of the specification and the cost of change.

Premature Acceptance of Other People's Software

Acceptance by a project of any internal or external subcontractor-developed software should be only conditional at the time of its own acceptance or validation tests. Final acceptance should be deferred if possible until successful completion of integrated system tests involving the subcontracted item. This is a particular problem in large projects, but can also occur even on small projects if implementation responsibility is split between groups.

The reader should not allow these horror stories to put him off. CM methodology, if applied with sufficient planning and common sense, can bring impressive results in both large and small organisations. Its increasing adoption in many software contexts is a sign of the growing maturity of the industry — a step from the alchemy of programming to the professional environment of the software engineer.

Appendix A Development CM Checklist

This list of questions is intended to provoke a project manager into discovering the areas of his project that need CM controls. It can be applied at any time during a project but preferably as early as possible (though some questions cannot be fully answered until later). Experience of using the checklist could well cause modifications or additions to it for subsequent projects. The subject area covered is much wider than pure CM requires and touches on the interaction of CM with other management and control methods.

A. Specifications

(1) Is there a *system specification*, that is, a document specifying the requirements for both hardware and software?
(2) Is there a *software functional specification*?
(3) Is there an overall *design document*; that is, an outline design of the system, including details of what pieces of existing systems are going to be used and the detailed specifications of the new modules? It should also contain details of structure, data, interfaces, etc.
(4) Do detailed design documents exist for each new piece?
(5) Are there any other relevant specification documents?
(6) For each specification, who is responsible for

- producing it?
- maintaining it?
- agreeing to alterations?

B. Test Requirements

(1) Is there a *system test requirements* document? That is, something that specifies what tests are needed, test data, expected results, etc.
(2) Are there *unit test requirements*? That is, similar items for each new unit of the system.
(3) Is there a schedule of acceptance tests?
(4) Are there any other test specifications?
(5) What standards of testing are imposed on code modules?
(6) For each document, who is responsible for

- producing it?
- maintaining it?
- agreeing to alterations?

C. Plans

(1) Is there an overall project plan?
(2) Are the *baselines* fully defined? Are the acceptance procedure and criteria for each defined?
(3) Is there a *build plan*? That is, a phased plan for producing several separate working versions with increasing functional capability?
(4) For each build (if there is more than one), is there a separate *integration plan* for putting all the components together?
(5) Are there *test plans*

- for each unit?
- for each build?

(6) Are there any other relevant plans?
(7) For each plan, who is responsible for

- producing it?
- maintaining it?
- agreeing to alterations?

D. Integration

(1) Who is responsible for integrating the pieces for each build?
(2) Once they are integrated, who can change them?
(3) Who validates the build? Against what criteria?
(4) How are errors found in new modules dealt with?
(5) How are errors found in existing subsystems dealt with?
(6) How are units accepted for integration?
(7) What procedures exist?

E. Reviews

(1) What design reviews, inspections, quality audits, etc., are carried out?
(2) How is conformity with standards monitored?
(3) Do checklists exist for review purposes?
(4) How are reviews followed up?
(5) Do all the participants realise their responsibilities?

F. Interfaces and Support

(1) How are interfaces with external contractors or users handled?

(2) How are interfaces with subcontractors or other internal development groups handled?
(3) Have the needs of production of more than one version of the system been taken into account?
(4) What support is to be given to users? Is there a plan for it?
(5) Is there an error handling system operational? Planned?
(6) Is there a defined interface with hardware or support staff?

G.   Documentation

(1) What internal and user documentation is produced?
(2) Who is responsible for it?
(3) Who validates user documentation? Maintenance documentation?
(4) Who can change documentation?
(5) Are records kept for each unit of the system?
(6) Is documentation kept on the computer? Could it be?
(7) How are changes in software tied to changes in documentation and vice versa?

H.   Change Control

(1) Is there any system for controlling and approving changes to any of the above plans, documents or software?
(2) Are records of changes kept?
(3) How is reporting against plans and budgets done?
(4) How are the effects of changes on schedules or budgets established and published?
(5) Are there any publications on this subject? Are all staff aware of them?

I.   Tools

(1) What language is the system written in?
(2) What tools are used in unit development (compiler, test harness, editor, etc.)? Are they all available and compatible?
(3) What method is used to store versions of units, listings, etc.?
(4) What tools are used in integration of units to make a build?
(5) What archives are kept? How?
(6) Is there a system for controlling changes to code? Is it enforced by tools?
(7) Could the tools be better integrated?

J.   Completion

(1) What constitutes completion of the project?
(2) What happens when the project is completed

● to the product?

- to the team?
- to the archives?

(3) Who will be responsible for maintaining the product?

K. Education

(1) Are the answers to each of the above questions adequately documented and known to all relevant project-associated staff?

Appendix B   Sample CM Procedures

This appendix contains sample procedures based on actual routines used in one or more installations known to the author. They are intended as a basis for the development of customised procedures for any particular organisation that wishes to introduce CM. Each will need adaptation to the environment, organisation and other control procedures in operation. Only a subset of those necessary to introduce the full CM methodology covered by the book are included. They should, however, be sufficient to give the flavour of the rest.

In general, it has been found that three short but interconnected procedures are easier to read, understand and introduce than one larger one. However, those presented here would probably require an 'overall CM procedure' establishing the context in which these would work.

Items in the procedures in square brackets [ ] are intended to be filled in by the person adapting them. The initial sections follow a standard format that has been found useful in practice. In usage, each procedure would have a cover sheet with a title and authorisation signatures, similar to the specification front sheet proposed in the first procedure. An example was given in figure 2.3.

The procedures included are

- CM1: Specification documents standards — standards for documentary baselines; this covers the areas discussed in section 5.1;
- CM2: Document creation and document change control — procedures for producing and maintaining baseline documents; corresponds to sections 5.2 and 5.3;
- CM3: Development documents — definitions of the actual documents produced in a medium-sized development project; corresponds to sections of chapter 3;
- CM4: Design inspections — a procedure defining I_1 Fagan inspections; corresponds to sections 7.2 and 7.3;
- CM5: Basis code and documentation control — a procedure for maintaining a developed system from which multiple versions are produced; corresponds to section 10.5; the basic code control method can be used in other circumstances, for example, development.

	DEVELOPMENT SPECIFICATION STANDARDS	CM1	
		Page 1	of 3
		Edition 1	Date 16.7.80

0   CONTENTS

1   SCOPE

2   REFERENCED DOCUMENTS

3   STAFF AFFECTED

4   SPECIFICATION FRONT SHEETS

5   SUBSEQUENT PAGES

1   SCOPE

In order that a standard change control and configuration management system can be introduced for product development it is essential that all specification documents pertaining to a particular product:

- are easily identifiable

- contain approval records

- contain status and date information.

A standard front sheet is specified to contain the relevant information. This must be provided for each of the <u>prime specification documents</u> mentioned in reference 2.2. It may also be used for any other documents if the author wishes.

2   REFERENCED DOCUMENTS

2.1 Development Document Creation and Change Control, reference CM2.

2.2 Development Documents, reference CM3.

3   STAFF AFFECTED

Authors of all prime specification documents.

4   SPECIFICATION FRONT SHEETS

All prime specification documents, as defined in reference 2.2 must have a front sheet consisting of a completed form jkbl. A completed example of this form is shown as Fig.5.1. This contains note numbers which refer to the following sub-sections. No prime specification document must appear without a front sheet.

The content of a completed front sheet is as follows:

4.1 <u>Ref</u>. ①

This is a unique reference number for the document, possibly in conjunction with 4.2 below. Space is also provided for numbering copies, if required.

4.2 <u>System</u> ②

The reference of the system being specified (may be omitted if this is completely covered by 4.4 below).

	DEVELOPMENT SPECIFICATION STANDARDS	CM1	
		Page 2	**of** 3
		Edition 1	**Date** 16.7.80

4.3 <u>Status</u> ③

This shows the status of acceptance of the document, by the checking of a colour code box. If more than one box is checked the highest status applies (e.g. in the example of Figure 5.1 the status is 'red'). The meaning of the colour codes is:

White: the document, which is not necessarily complete, is circulated for comment or early information.

Green: the document is circulated for approval by the approval authorities (see below).

Red: the document has been accepted by the approval authorities and is now under change control (see references 2.1 and 2.2).

4.4 <u>Title</u> ④

The title of the specification. This may, but need not, be followed by a contents list.

4.5 <u>Distribution</u> ⑤

The distribution list for the specification. Red status versions of prime specification documents have a mandatory distribution list; extra recipients are also allowed at the author's discretion. The mandatory distribution list consists of the change approval authorities plus a standard Reader List.

4.6 <u>Issue</u> ⑥

Issues of a document are numbered sequentially, starting at 1. Each reissue with a change causes the issue number to be increased by 1, unless the only change is to the colour status. Information on previous issues is retained on the cover sheet. In the example the current document is issue 3. If the issue number rises above six a new front sheet must be produced but the old sheet should be retained as a record. See also 4.10 below. Note that if a subsequent page is not changed in a reissue it may, but need not, retain its previous version number. An issue, unlike an amendment (see 4.10), always contains all the pages of the document.

4.7 <u>Date</u> ⑦

The date of issue of this version.

4.8 <u>Prepared</u> ⑧

The name or initials of the author of the specification.

4.9 <u>Approved</u> ⑨

One of these columns is used by each of the Approval Authorities for the document - see reference 2.1. Each

	DEVELOPMENT SPECIFICATION STANDARDS	(a) (b) (c)	CM1	
			Page · 3	**of** 3
			Edition 1	**Date** 16.7.80

(d)

authority indicates approval by signing or initialling the relevant box. Red status documents will have a signature here for each of the Approval Authorities.

4.10　Amendment　(10)

For large documents an amendment may be made by the issue of a single sheet or collection of sheets rather than a complete reissue of a document. Such amendments are numbered sequentially starting at 1 for each issue. Each amendment normally has its own front sheet on a form, jkb1. The issue number (4.6) will be the same as the previous issue but an amendment number will be specified in this column. If several amendments are concatenated or circulated together several numbers may be stated here. Changes to red status documents must be approved by the approval authorities before they become effective.

4.11　Pages　(11)

The number of pages in this issue or amendment. This entry is optional and local standards may be employed (e.g. number to include/exclude appendices, front sheet numbered 0 or 1, etc.)

5　　SUBSEQUENT PAGES

Subsequent pages should use form jkb2 (i.e. this form) and each page should contain the following information - Notes refer to the top of this page:

-　document reference　(a)

-　page number　(b)

-　issue number (plus amendment number if any - e.g. 1/2)　(c)

-　date　(d)

Note that the issue number of a page may be less than or equal to the document issue number. Unchanged pages from previous document issues do not need to have their page issue number changed.

The following standard sections should be used at the start of any specification document (unless the description in reference 2.2 states otherwise).

0　　Contents

1　　Scope (a brief outline of the contents and purpose of the document.

2　　Document History

2.1　　Changes from previous version

2.2　　Future changes forecast

3　　Referenced Documents

Sections 4 onwards contain the specification proper which may also be standardised for particular specification types.

		CM2	
	DEVELOPMENT DOCUMENT CREATION	**Page** 1	**of** 6
	& CHANGE CONTROL	**Edition** 1	**Date** 16.7.80

0   CONTENTS

     1   SCOPE

     2   REFERENCED DOCUMENTS

     3   STAFF AFFECTED

     4   PRODUCING DOCUMENTS FOR CHANGE CONTROL

     5   CHANGING RED DOCUMENTS

     6   COMPLETING A SPECIFICATION CHANGE PROPOSAL

     7   APPROVING CHANGES

     APPENDIX B - Change Proposal Form.

1   SCOPE

"Producing a system from a specification is like walking on water: it's easier if it's frozen " - B. Boehm.

This procedure specifies the methods for producing, agreeing and controlling changes to specification documents. It ensures that:

-   all relevant parties are consulted before documents or changes are agreed

-   there is an early exchange of information

-   costs of changes can be assessed before the change is made.

The procedure is obligatory for all prime specification documents as defined in reference 2.2. It may also be used for other documents. Reference 2.1 defines concepts such as 'colour status', which are used in this procedure. The general operations of the procedure are shown in Figure 5.3 as an SADT diagram.

Actual document production remains as informal as possible and the procedure is mainly concerned with eliminating oversights and recording decisions.

2   REFERENCED DOCUMENTS

2.1   Development Specification Standards, reference CM1.

2.2   Development Documents, reference CM3.

3   STAFF AFFECTED

The procedure affects all staff who produce, approve or use specification documents. Each prime specification document has:

-   an originator (or author)

-   approval authorities

-   a reader list.

These are defined in references 2.1 and 2.2. Each plays a distinct role as described in subsequent sections. The

	DEVELOPMENT DOCUMENT CREATION & CHANGE CONTROL	CM2		
		Page 2	of 6	
		Edition 1	Date 16.7.80	

documents covered by this procedure are described more fully in reference 2.2.

4   PRODUCING DOCUMENTS FOR CHANGE CONTROL

A flow chart for the steps necessary to produce a document and place it under change control is given as Figure 5.4. It should be examined together with Figure 5.3, which shows the relationships of the originator, approval authorities and reader list.

4.1   Initial Steps

The originator should establish personal contact with the approval authorities for the document and discuss content, timescales and any special problems. It will also be necessary to examine and understand associated documentation, e.g. the content of a system development specification will control the production of much of the software design specification. This stage may require detailed interaction, e.g. with technical experts within the team, sales and customer representatives, etc.

4.2   Producing Drafts

The originator produces a draft of the document. If the document contains areas likely to cause disagreement, or if the timescales involved are long, one or more white status versions should be produced and circulated to both the approval authorities and the reader lists. White status versions may also be sent to more limited lists to obtain information and check understanding. White status documents need not be complete.

Close personal contact should be maintained at this stage between the originator and approval authorities so that formal approval becomes as far as possible a "rubber stamp" operation. Production of white versions continues until the originator has a draft which:

a)   is complete

b)   he supports, and

c)   he believes he has a good chance of being accepted.

4.3   Seeking Approval

When a draft satisfying (a), (b) and (c) of 4.2 is available it is published as a green status document, with a request for approval. It is the originator's responsibility to try to obtain agreement from the authorities. If this is not forthcoming, he may make changes until either approval is obtained, in which case a red status document is published, or a deadlock is reached. Formal approval should normally be given at a meeting of the approval authorities after the document has been made available for study.

	DEVELOPMENT DOCUMENT CREATION & CHANGE CONTROL	CM2		
		Page 3	**of** 6	
		Edition 1	**Date** 16.7.80	

4.4   <u>Resolving Deadlocks</u>

If a deadlock occurs, the problem should be referred to higher authority as defined in reference 2.2.

4.5   <u>Publishing a Red Status Document</u>

When agreement is assured, a red status document is produced and agreement is signified by the signatures on the cover sheet of the document. A red status document is "frozen", i.e. it is subject to change control.

4.6   <u>Maintaining Frozen Documentation</u>

The responsibility for archiving red status documents rests with the originator. It is also the originator's responsibility to retain any working documentation made during the production of the document, particularly that relating to reasons for particular decisions.

5   CHANGING RED DOCUMENTS

This section refers only to change control during the development period. After handover documents are subject to maintenance change control procedures. A flow chart of the operation is given as Figure 5.5.

Red status documents may require changes; this is allowed but only under strict control. Possible reasons for a change are:

- errors discovered in the system documented

- errors in the document itself

- changes made in associated documents

- improvements requested to specifications.

5.1   <u>System Errors</u>

The first class normally occur during testing or validation and it must be possible to change the code immediately to prevent delays. However, strict control is then necessary to ensure that corresponding changes are made to the affected documentation. This is done by completion of a specification change proposal - see 6 below.

5.2   <u>Specification Errors</u>

If anyone discovers an error or omission in a red status specification document, he should raise a specification change proposal. This covers both mismatches between a document and the system, mismatches between various specifications, or areas of specification documents which make implementation difficult or impossible. Note particularly that such changes may affect more than one document; for example, a change to a system specification may in turn require a change to the software specification. Change proposals for all such documents should be raised simultaneously, to each of the relevant authorities.

	DEVELOPMENT DOCUMENT CREATION & CHANGE CONTROL	CM2	
		Page 4	**of** 6
		Edition 1	**Date** 16.7.80

5.3   Improvements

If anyone requires an improvement or other change to an approved specification it must be done by raising the necessary change proposal(s).

6   COMPLETING A SPECIFICATION CHANGE PROPOSAL

A change proposal is completed on a standard form jkb3. An example of a completed form is shown in Figure 5.6. Each of the following sections refers to a box to be completed.

6.1   CP Number

The number of this change proposal. Change proposals for a document will be numbered sequentially and the document originator will keep track of which numbers have been issued, approved etc. and provide a CP number to the raiser of a proposal on request. The person raising a change proposal must therefore obtain a number from the document originator.

6.2   Document Reference

The reference of the document which has to be changed, together with its issue number.

6.3   Date

The date of the completion of the form.

6.4   Change Raised By

The name of the person completing the change proposal form.

6.5   Project

The name of the project.

6.6   Other Affected Documents

The names or reference numbers of any other documents which need corresponding changes. All such changes should be considered together and approval given by joint operation of the relevant approval bodies.

6.7   Other Affected Projects

Other items requiring corresponding changes. All such changes should be considered together. As an example a change to a library routine may have an effect on several software items.

6.8   Reasons for Change

There are four reasons for change and one of the appropriate boxes should be checked:

a)   The system needs correction to function properly and this affects the documentation. If this box is checked

	DEVELOPMENT DOCUMENT CREATION & CHANGE CONTROL	CM2	
		Page 5	**of** 6
		Edition 1	**Date** 16.7.80

a reference should be given to the validation report, error report, usability report, note etc. which stated the need for the change. In this type of change the urgency may have caused the correction to be made before the proposal was raised. The appropriate box for this should be checked and if 'yes', a reference given for the issued change.

b)   There is an error in the specification which needs to be put right. Again, the reference of any letter, memo. etc. reporting the error should be stated.

c)   A user or project member has requested an improvement. If this box is checked, the reference of the document making such a request must be quoted. It must also be stated if the change affects finances or timescales, if this is known, in which case details are given below.

d)   For any other reason give details.

6.9   Description of Change

Specifies the change(s) needed to the document, using continuation sheets if necessary.

6.10   Consequences of Change

This section is for specifying such items as delays to time-scales, extra costs etc. which need to be considered by the change approval authorities, and consequences of not changing.

6.11   Authority

If the scope of the change is outside the limit of authority of the document approval body, this box should be ticked. However, the change must also be presented to the normal approval body for their consideration. This is to cover a case where, for example, a code change can give rise to a facility change affecting higher level documents than the current one.

6.12   Approval Authorities

These must be the approval authorities for the original document plus the document originator.

6.13   Further Distribution

All others apart from the approval list, to whom the change should be sent. This should include at least all the recipients of the document to be changed.

6.14   Comments

Can be used for notes, approval signatures or action records.

	DEVELOPMENT DOCUMENT CREATION & CHANGE CONTROL	CM2	
		Page 6	**of** 6
		Edition 1	**Date** 16.7.80

7   APPROVING CHANGES

The method for approving changes is very similar to that for establishing red status documents. The operations are included in the SADT diagram of Figure 5.3, and Figure 5.5 shows a flow chart for the following sections.

7.1   Agreeing a Change Proposal

A change proposal is completed and circulated as described in section 6. If agreement to the change can be obtained from all relevant parties a document amendment can be prepared immediately. The responsibility for obtaining agreement to the change proposals lies with the person raising it and he must make any modifications necessary to obtain approval. If it is decided that the change should not be made the CP is withdrawn (but still registered and filed).

7.2   Resolving Deadlocks

The deadlock resolution procedure is the same as for new documents. Changes outside the authority of the approval group must be raised in a similar manner.

7.3   Amending a Document

Once a change proposal has been accepted, it is the responsibility of the originator(s) of the document(s) to make the relevant changes. This can be done in a number of ways:

a)   If the change if a major one the document can be amended and completely reissued. The issue number will be increased by one and the document will be reissued with red status and appropriate signatures - see reference 2.1.

b)   If the change is not major but has a significant effect on the document, individual pages may be reissued together with a new front sheet as an amendment to the specification - see reference 2.1. Amendments to a given issue are numbered sequentially starting at 1 and each amended page should be marked with:

        <issue number>/<amendment number>

c)   If the change is minor a description of the change may be issued as an amendment. This could, for example, consist only of the change proposal itself with an appropriate amendment front sheet.

Amendments or reissues must be sent to all recipients of the original document. Responsibility for filing new issues, previous issues and change proposals rests with the originator. The project leader is responsible for ensuring that any subsequent related action (e.g. correction of code) is planned and carried out.

	DEVELOPMENT DOCUMENTS	CM3	
		Page 1	**of** 4
		Edition 1	**Date** 16.7.80

0   CONTENTS

1   SCOPE

2   REFERENCED DOCUMENTS

3   STAFF AFFECTED

4   DOCUMENT BASELINES

    4.1   Project start

    4.2   User requirements specification

    4.3   System development specification

    4.4   Design specifications

    4.5   Detailed design and implementation

    4.6   Handover documents

    4.7   User manuals

    4.8   The product specification.

5   PRODUCING BASELINE DOCUMENTS

6   DOCUMENT CHANGE CONTROL

7   REPORTING

ATTACHMENT A - Document Descriptions

ATTACHMENT B - Figure

1   SCOPE

This document describes in outline specification baseline
control systems for development projects. The procedure is
relevant to completely new products or major changes to
existing products. Together with the related procedures of
section 2 and those defining review boards, see reference [   ]
it describes a complete documentation system for development
projects which covers:

-    definition of the documents which form controlled baselines
     in development projects, their contents and
     responsibilities for authoring, approval and change.

-    methods of producing such documents to standard formats
     and getting them agreed.

-    methods of changing such documents under control.

-    a description of the approval and change committees for
     various documents, their relationships, responsibilities,
     authorities and organisation.

2   REFERENCED DOCUMENTS

2.1   Inspection teams, reference CM4

2.2   Development Document Creation and Change Control, reference
       CM2.

2.3   Development Specification Standards, reference CM1.

		CM3	
[logo]	DEVELOPMENT DOCUMENTS	**Page** 2	**of** 4
		Edition 1	**Date** 16.7.80

2.4   Steering Committees and Review Boards, reference [   ]

3   STAFF AFFECTED

All staff concerned in development and maintenance will be affected in some way.

4   DOCUMENT BASELINES

All development programmes will incorporate baselines through-out the project.   Early baselines are marked by the publication and <u>approval</u> of specified documents;   later base-lines cover the availability of developed hardware or code. Diagrams of the development programme are shown in Figures 2.2, and 3.4.   A simplified version for the purposes of this procedure is shown in Attachment B.   The baseline points and corresponding documents considered by this procedure are listed in the following sections.   Detailed descriptions of the documents or references to where they can be found are given in Attachment A;   brief descriptions follow here.   Note that for small projects documents may be concatenated, e.g. 4.3 and 4.4 could form separate sections of a single document. Conversely, for very large developments 4.3 could be expanded into a number of subsystem Development Specifications.

The following list should be taken as standard.   Any deviations would need to be agreed by the Project Steering Committee.

4.1   <u>Project Start</u>

The start of a project, for the purposes of this procedure, is the approval of a project and the assignment of resources. The detailed form of the initiation documents or the criteria and methods by which approval is obtained are not the concern of this procedure.   However, a preliminary user requirements specification is normally needed before approval is given.

4.2   <u>User Requirements Specification</u>

The agreement of this document, which is produced by or in conjunction with users, and defines the functions and performance of the project and an outline of how the system works in user terms, constitutes the achievement of the first baseline, B1.   Approval is given and changes controlled by a review board.

4.3   <u>System Development Specification</u>

This document, produced by the development team, defines the functions of the product from an implementation viewpoint and is the basis for the development phase which follows keypoint B1.   Hardware changes and software are covered.   This document shows how each of the subsystems are connected to form a system which satisfies the user requirements specification. Approval and change control is by a review board.

	DEVELOPMENT DOCUMENTS	CM3		
		Page 3	**of** 4	
		Edition 1	**Date** 16.7.80	

4.4 Design Specifications

These contain detailed descriptions of the systems down to a 'component' level, and definitions of the way the subsystems work together. Test requirements are also specified for each. If hardware changes are required installation specifications will be produced in a similar way. Approval and change control is by a review board.

4.5 Detailed Design/Implementation Documents

These exist for each new software item. In most cases these documents are reviewed and approved by inspection team (see reference 2.1). Acceptance of these and testing of the corresponding software constitute baseline B4 (although this may be a series of events rather than a single point).

4.6 Handover Documents

These consist of updated versions of all previous documents plus the information necessary to allow hardware production and production manuals for customized software. Acceptance of the documents and the product itself after suitable validation constitutes the handover to maintenance, baseline B5.

4.7 User Manuals

In parallel with software development, user manuals and specific maintenance documentation is produced. These form part of the handover documentation and will be inspected (see reference 2.1).

4.8 The Product Specification

This is not a baseline document, but an index to each of the above baseline documents. It forms the top level of the hierarchy of documentation which is handed over to maintenance at the end of development. Interim versions of the product specification are produced throughout the development period to provide a reference to the currently available baselines.

5 PRODUCING BASELINE DOCUMENTS

Prime Specification documents are produced using standard formats and standard contents lists. These standards are referenced in Attachment A. Approval of each of these documents is by a nominated review board with representatives of all relevant parties.

6 DOCUMENT CHANGE CONTROL

Change control during the development period is carried out according to the procedure of reference 2.2. The approval authorities and the change control authorities in all technical areas for the baseline documents are the relevant review boards. However, if changes involve financial deviations or major functional changes at the user level, or if the review board

	DEVELOPMENT DOCUMENTS	CM3	
		Page 4	**of** 4
		Edition 1	**Date** 16.7.80

cannot agree, the matter is referred up to the project steering committee for the product.

All changes, whatever their type, are always submitted to the review board first and then passed up, with appropriate technical briefing for high level review if necessary. Connected changes are always put forward together. Changes which affect more than one document are submitted simultaneously to both review boards who act as a single body for consideration of the change. Change control after completion of the development is not the concern of this procedure.

7   REPORTING

The project manager is responsible for reporting the successful completion of baselines to the steering committee and the successful completion of approved changes to the review boards and the steering committee.

	ATTACHMENT A Document Descriptions	CM3		
		Page A-1	of 2	
		Edition 1		Date 16.7.80

[This attachment should list for every controlled baseline document needed during a development project, either the following information or an indication of where the information can be found if it is published separately:

- the document name
- the document reference
- a description of the document
- a list of contents
- the people responsible for the production, maintenance, review, approval and change control of the document throughout the development period
- standards to which the document conforms
- notes on the document

These are so project-dependent that only one example is given here to form a template. It is to be expected that most medium-sized developments would have entries for the following:

- product specifications
- project initiation documents
- user requirements specifications
- system development specifications
- software design specifications (in this issue)
- hardware configuration and installation specifications
- programmer notebooks

- test descriptions
- software maintenance guides
- verification reports
- handover documentation]

A1   SOFTWARE DESIGN SPECIFICATION

A1.1 Description

This document describes the design of the software system, and identifies its structure down to the level of implementable components, for which specifications are given.

A1.2 Reference

The reference of a software design specification is of the form: [   ]

A1.3 Contents

0   Contents List

1   Scope: Introduction to the document

	ATTACHMENT A Document Descriptions	CM3	
		Page A-2	of 2
		Edition 1	Date 16.7.80

  2 Document history

    2.1 Changes from previous version

    2.2 Changes forecast

  3 Referenced documents

  4 Software system structure

  5 List of software modules

  6 Module specifications:
    Separate sections for each module giving:

       − the module name (and unit name if modules are collected in units)

       − interface definitions

       − purpose

       − algorithms   )
) outline only - details are in
       − test descriptions) Programmer Notebooks

       − references to data used

  7 Data definitions and layout

  8 Test descriptions:

    for subsystems and total software system.

A1.4 <u>Responsibility</u>

    Originator: the project leader

    Readers: nominated representatives of a development team, users, maintainers.

    Approval Authorities: Software Design Review Board.

    Standards: conforms to reference 2.3 and to any design standards stated in the system development specification.

A1.5 <u>Notes</u>

This document answers the question "How is the software made?" Design languages or graphics can be used for section 4 and for individual specifications of complex modules. Flow charts and/or pseudocode can be employed for section 6, where relevant. Section 6 and parts of sections 7 and 8 form the basis of the programmer notebooks for each module and can be produced initially in that form if required.

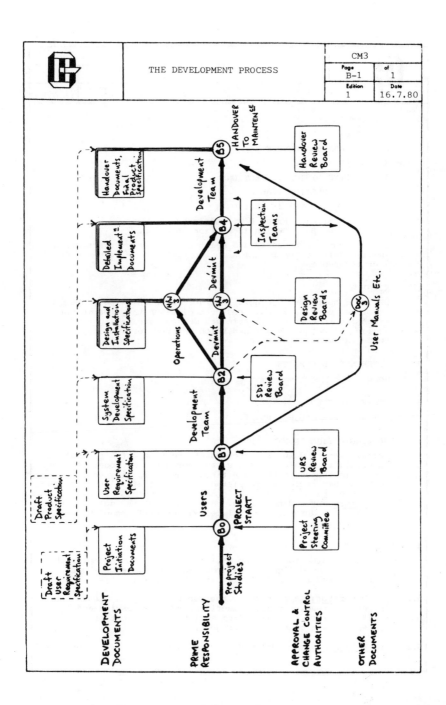

	DESIGN INSPECTIONS	CM4	
		Page 1	of 3
		Edition 1	Date 16.7.80

0   CONTENTS

[Attachments to be added and maintained as inspections are used.
Initial entries for brackets in the text can be found in Chapter
7 or reference 9]

1   SCOPE

Design inspections are held in order to catch as many design
errors as possible before coding begins and they become more
expensive to correct. A standard method of carrying out the
design inspection is defined which has been proved in practice
to be extremely cost-effective.

2   REFERENCED DOCUMENTS

None.

3   STAFF AFFECTED

All software project staff.

4   HOLDING DESIGN INSPECTIONS

Normally one module is inspected at one time but with small
interrelated modules with the same designer and coder, several
can be inspected at the same time. The design inspection will
be held when design is completed to a level at which code blocks
of between [   ] and [   ] source statements can be isolated
and before any coding begins. At this point the designer will
inform the moderator (see 5.1 below) who will organise the
inspections.

5   THE INSPECTION TEAM

A design inspection will normally consist of four people: the
moderator, the designer, the coder and the tester. Their
functions and responsibilities are as follows:

5.1   The Moderator: appointed by the project manager. Leads the
        inspection team, schedules meetings, reports results and
        monitors rework. Usually from a different project or a
        different part of the same project.

5.2   The Designer: the person who designed the item being inspected.

	DESIGN INSPECTIONS	CM4	
		Page 2	**of** 3
		Edition 1	**Date** 16.7.80

5.3   <u>The Coder</u>: the person who is to code the item, or if the
       designer is to code it, a programmer from another part of the
       project or a related project.

5.4   <u>The Tester</u>:   the person who is to produce the test cases for
       the item or if this is the designer or coder, a programmer from
       another part of the project or a related project.

       Designers of other system parts with which the item interfaces
       may also attend.

6   CONDUCT OF THE INSPECTIONS

       The moderator will schedule meetings for the inspections,
       preferably in two-hour sessions, once or twice a day.
       Approximately [ ] man hours per 1000 lines of code should be
       allowed including rework time by the designer. The inspection
       consists of five phases as follows:

6.1   <u>Overview</u>

       The designer presents the overall design of the project area
       which includes the item and then the detailed design of the
       item. Design documentation is then distributed. Particular
       attention is given to any specification changes made during the
       design phase.

6.2   <u>Individual Preparation</u>

       Team members try to understand the design individually. The
       checklists of error distribution and questions to ask contained
       in Attachment A and B are useful here.

6.3   <u>Formal Inspection</u>

       The whole team meet to inspect the design. The coder presents
       the design as he understands it. Every piece of logic and
       every possible branch must be considered at least once and all
       available documentation studied.

       All errors discovered are noted by the moderator together with
       solutions if they are obvious. However, <u>no time is spent
       searching for solutions or discussing alternatives to the design</u>

       At the end of the formal inspection, the moderator produces,
       <u>within one day</u>, a written report. This is given to all
       attendees at the inspection, plus:
       [   ]
       to allow updating of the checklists of Attachments A and B.

6.4   <u>Rework</u>

       All errors discovered are corrected by the designer.

6.5   <u>Follow-up</u>

       The moderator satisfies himself that all the rework has been

		CM4	
	DESIGN INSPECTIONS	**Page** 3	**of** 3
		Edition 1	**Date** 16.7.80

done. If this involves more than [ ]% of the design a
complete new inspection should be held. Otherwise, the
inspection team may be reconvened to study the rework only,
or for trivial changes the moderator alone may check it.

	BASIS CODE AND DOCUMENTATION CHANGE CONTROL	CM5		
		Page 1	of	2
		Edition 1	Date 16.7.80	

0   CONTENTS

1   SCOPE

2   REFERENCED DOCUMENTS

3   STAFF AFFECTED

4   CHANGE PROCEDURE

Sample change request form.

1   SCOPE

The purpose of this routine is to establish controllable ways of introducing changes (fault corrections, new features etc.) in the basis software package and its documentation.

2   REFERENCED DOCUMENTS

None.

3   STAFF AFFECTED

The Change Committee for basis code and documentation consists of representatives from:
[   ]

The first of these is the convenor of the committee. Other representatives may be involved in specific meetings.

4   CHANGE PROCEDURE

4.1   Detecting a basis error

When a basis error or need for an amendment is found, the person responsible for this particular system shall first try to find a solution, if necessary after consulting others involved.

4.2   Error reporting

When the solution is found, the section marked "Proposer" on the change request form must be filled out and the left hand set of boxes ticked where relevant. The form is then sent to the convenor of the committee.

Error reports may be sent without proposed solutions, but this should be avoided if possible.

4.3   Change Committee handling

When an error report is received by the convenor it is given a registered file number, and it is archived in the change request file.

Change Committee meetings will be held depending on the frequency of incoming reports. Normally, this meeting should be held at least [   ].

The Change Committee is responsible for the following

		CM5	
	BASIS CODE AND DOCUMENTATION CHANGE CONTROL	**Page** 2	**of** 2
		Edition 1	**Date** 16.7.80

decisions:

a) Should the change be implemented or rejected?

b) Is more information needed? If so, who is responsible for obtaining it?

c) If it is to be implemented, what priority should be assigned?

d) Must documentation be updated?

e) Must the testing procedures be updated?

f) Is reissue necessary for one or more user systems?

g) Should users be informed?

h) Should the problem be raised to higher levels?

Appropriate indications are made on the form, using the right hand set of boxes and comment areas.

If the reported solution is to be implemented as a basis correction, the document is given a correction number and a copy is archived in the special correction file for processing.

4.4 Subsequent Action

A meeting report from the Change Committee should immediately be written and distributed to:

    [   ]

and all people concerned and who are involved in further action. It should be accompanied by copies of the completed change request forms.

Updated documentation must be distributed to all relevant parties as soon as possible.

Subsequent meetings of the change committee should monitor the process of all approved changes and when complete, indicate the applicable correction in the bottom right hand box.

ATTACHMENT A TO PROCEDURE CM5

	BASIS SOFTWARE AND DOCUMENTATION CHANGE REQUEST	Reg.No.
		Date

PROPOSER

PROJECT/PRODUCT:
STATUS:

CHANGE INITIATED BY:
DEPARTMENT:

WHY CHANGE? (Problem description, consequences of changing and/or not changing)

HOW CHANGE? (Proposed change(s) and alternatives)

CHANGE COMMITTEE

ESTIMATED COST OF CHANGE:
Small <1MW
Medium <4MW
Large >4MW

P CC

CHANGE PROPOSAL VERIFIED BY:
Lab. trials
System at customer
Know-how
Not verified

P CC

PROBLEM ANALYSIS:
Catastrophic failure
Functional error
Functional Problem
Documentation faulty

CONSEQUENCES FOR:
Specifications
Documentation
Production procedures
Acceptance tests
Hardware

CORRECTIVE ACTION:
Implemented ASAP
Better verification
Rejected
Documentation to be
  updated

Test proc.to be updated
Reissue necessary
Customers to be informed
Raised to higher
  authority

APPROVAL AUTHORITIES:

COMMENTS:

FURTHER DISTRIBUTION:

CORRECTION NUMBER:

References and Bibliography

1 B. W. Boehm *et al.*, *Development and Configuration Management Manual*, TRW-SS-73-07 (December 1973).
2 J. K. Buckle, *Managing Software Projects* (MacDonald and Jane's, 1977).
3 SofTech Inc., *An Introduction to SADT*, Document No. 9022-78R.
4 D. T. Ross and K. E. Schoman, Structured Analysis for Requirements Definition, in *Proceedings of Second International Conference on Software Engineering* (October 1976).
5 M. Lundeberg *et al.*, A Systematic Approach to Information Systems Development, *Information Systems*, 4, Nos. 1 and 2.
6 J. K. Buckle, Requirements for Effective Analysis Standards, in *Proceedings of IAG Workshop on Standards for Systems Analysis* (March 1980).
7 M. Rochkind, The Source Code Control System, *IEEE Trans. Software Engng*, SE-1 (December 1975).
8 J. T. Pedersen and J. K. Buckle, Kongsberg's Road to an Industrial Software Methodology, *IEEE Trans. Software Engng*, **SE-4** (July 1978).
9 M. E. Fagan, Design and Code Inspection to Reduce Errors in Program Development, *IBM Syst. J.*, **15**, No. 3 (1976).
10 NCC, *Data Processing Documentation Standards* (NCC, 1978).
11 A. Irvine and J. W. Brackett, Automated Software Engineering, through Structured Data Management, *IEEE Trans. Software Engng* (January 1977).
12 Cap-Sogeti-Logiciel, *Memento de la Methodologie* (CSL, 1978).
13 S. Eanes *et al.*, An Environment for Producing Well-engineered Microcomputer Software, in *Proceedings of Fourth International Conference on Software Engineering* (Munich, 1979).
14 B. W. Kernighan and K. R. Mashey, The UNIX Programming Environment, *Software Practice and Experience*, 9 (1979).
15 S. I. Feldman, Make — A Program for Maintaining Computer Programs, *Bell Laboratories Report* (August 1978).
16 D. E. Hall, D. K. Scherrer and J. S. Sventek, A Virtual Operating System, *Communs ACM* (September 1980).
17 B. W. Boehm, An Experiment in Small-scale Application Software Engineering, *IEEE Trans Software Engng*, **SE-7** (September 1981).
18 E. Yourdon, *Structured Walkthroughs* (Yourdon Press, 1977).

The following books and articles, while not referenced directly in the text, provide an interesting insight into the history and applications of configuration management, particularly in the US military area. The first also gives a comprehensive bibliography.

Bersoff, E. H. Henderson, V. D., and Siegel, S. G., 'Software Configuration Management: A Tutorial', *Computer* (January 1979).
Czerwinski, F. L., and Samaras, T. T., *Fundamentals of Configuration Management* (Wiley, 1971), chapter 21 is devoted to program CM.

McCarthy, R., Applying the Techniques of Configuration Management, *Defense Management Journal*, 11, No. 4 (October 1975).

Proceedings of the Life Cycle Management Conference, presented by the AIIE Washington 1977, Management Education Corporation.

Index